PRACTICAL SHOWING

NIGEL HOLLINGS

PRACTICAL SHOWING

Photographs by Bob Langrish

DAVID & CHARLES
Newton Abbot   London

I would like to thank my brother Stuart,
father George and fiancée Penny
for all the help they have given me
in preparing this book.

Photographs by Bob Langrish except where otherwise acknowledged

British Library Cataloguing in Publication Data

Hollings, Nigel
   Practical showing
   1. Livestock: Horses. Showing
   I. Title
   636.1'6

   ISBN 0-7153-9327-8

Typeset in Bembo by Typesetters (Birmingham) Ltd
Smethwick, West Midlands
and printed in Great Britain
by Redwood Burn Limited, Trowbridge, Wilts
for David & Charles Publishers plc
Brunel House   Newton Abbot   Devon

Contents

Foreword

Showing is an important part of an expanding equestrian industry, and is a vast subject. I firmly believe that it is attention to detail which achieves success in the show ring, so in the same way I have chosen to concentrate on particular aspects of showing which have not yet been examined in book form – therefore more general management (eg concerning ailments) is not within the scope of this book.

I have been lucky enough to meet and to train with some exceptionally talented personalities from whom I have learned a great deal, and this has given me a broader outlook on showing altogether. I myself always keep in mind a couple of golden rules: it pays to keep an open mind, as you are continually adding something to your knowledge; and you are only as successful as the animals that you produce. At the end of the day, as with judges and judging, production for the ring is a matter of opinion. With this in mind I have written this book in the hope it will be both interesting and informative – but also at times amusing, because without a sense of humour you will not survive in the showing game.

Nigel Hollings

The author aged twelve years old on Snailwell Charles, Pony of the Year, 1972, and winner of the 13.2hh Pony of the Year, 1973, with the 1972 conformation judge Colonel Dan Corry

CHAPTER 1

An Introduction to Showing

Horse shows are very much part of the British summer scene, although the term 'summer' can be used only very loosely when I recall some of the appalling weather conditions experienced over the last few seasons – it is hardly surprising that the waterproof clothing industry is a very profitable concern! The show season proper seems to get under way earlier every year; in fact many of the show pony exhibitors have already made a start at the indoor shows well before their WHP/SHP (working hunter pony/show hunter pony) colleagues have finished their winter season, which culminates in the Winter Championships at Stoneleigh in April.

THE SHOWING SEASON

The big outdoor show circuit usually starts with Ayr or Newark, depending on which part of the country you live in, and then the race to qualify for the Royal International Horse Show (RIHS) begins; there is no time to spare. This urgency is because the RIHS has been moved forward to June (previously it was held at Wembley in mid-July), so the first period of the show season has a life-span of only seven weeks and this creates its own problems. At one point there was talk of having some qualifying shows at the end of the previous season to reduce the intense atmosphere and the January sales-type rush.

Every exhibitor these days hopes to qualify all his animals very early on in the season; this reduces the pressure and also allows him to travel to the shows that he really enjoys, just like the good old days before qualification for the RIHS was introduced. An RIHS or Wembley qualification ticket can increase the value of an animal and make it more saleable, so it is highly advantageous to achieve this goal. However, many of the seasoned exhibitors feel that the fun element is lost when competing at this pace and pressure, and that this leads to animals being overshown and overtravelled too early in the year – no wonder some animals look

Horse shows are very much a part of the British summer scene

like shadows of their former selves towards the end of the season. Luckily the conveyor belt does at times grind to a halt; many exhibitors get a chance to enjoy a well deserved rest after the Horse of the Year Show in early October. But how I do envy the people who neither need nor want to join the race, and instead compete solely for pleasure.

The British Show Pony Society (BSPS) winter season is primarily aimed at the WHP/SHP exhibitors who wish to bring on their novices slowly during the quieter months in preparation for bigger challenges the following summer; its atmosphere is totally different. Absolutely everything ticks along at a smoother, quieter pace although the championship show is just as prestigious as the show pony, hack and hunter equivalents.

Showing is booming, despite the increasing cost of basic feedstuffs, travelling and entry fees (unfortunately prize money has not increased sufficiently to be considered a help) – you only need to see the fancy horseboxes, and the catalogues bursting with entries to know that this is true. Who would have believed twenty years ago that it was possible to have ninety-plus entries in some show classes?

FACTS AND FIGURES

The British Show Pony Society (BSPS) has a present-day membership of over 2,500 adult members, 2,000 junior members and 3,000 registered ponies. It also runs two major annual championship shows and has over 500 affiliated shows.

The British Show Hack, Cob and Riding Horse Association (BSHC & RH Association) has a present-day adult membership of about 1,000, and 160 junior members; there are about 800 registered horses, over 350 of which are riding horses, and the association runs 130 affiliated shows.

The Hunter Improvement Society (HIS) has a total membership of approximately 6,500, and in 1988 the show horse register totalled 976.

PEOPLE IN SHOWING

Competition in showing is very strong and there is no room for slap-dash attitudes – you only get out what you put in, whatever your level of competition. Outsiders do not always realise how much work is involved behind the scenes since they usually only see the finished product in the show ring, and if you do attempt to explain, especially mentioning the unearthly hour at which you left your comfortable bed to travel several hours along the motorway, then they begin to question your sanity – I must admit I have often questioned mine!

Showing means different things to different people: to the enthusiast it is a way of life, rather than a hobby which occupies just a few hours of each week. For some it is the chance to have a day out with the many friends it is possible to make in showing. For others it is the realisation of an ambition to own a champion which brings that sense of real achievement – sometimes succeeding where others have failed. The role of the professional and the breeder in the showing world is to maintain standards, and the show ring is their shop window; this will create other business opportunities which will, in turn, hopefully pay the bills. For the amateur, who is the backbone of the sport, it is an opportunity to compete against and often beat the experts at their own game.

An amusing situation exists between amateurs and professionals: the amateurs envy the professionals, thinking that they are difficult to beat, and that they would love to be in their position; whereas the professionals envy the amateurs and dream of the day when they can afford to concentrate on just one or two exhibits like the amateur. Another observation is that life at the top is lonely: everybody is your friend – but only when you aren't winning!

At the end of the day, life is what you make of it: very rarely

The show ring is the professionals' 'shop window'

does success fall into your lap, and in showing you have to be dedicated not only to succeed but to survive – Mrs Eckley, owner of the famous Cusop Stud, once said that the only profit you make is the enjoyment you receive! Nevertheless, one of the more pleasant aspects of showing is that you will meet many people from all walks of life who share your aim – to win with the perfect animal – and some of these people will become your lifelong friends. There is a great camaraderie, which in theory is surprising since you are usually competing against each other and especially as many people are not always at their best on the showfield – very often highly-strung and short-tempered. However, no-one will ever see you stuck for anything, whether you have forgotten a bridle, need help leading a foal in a championship or if your lorry needs a push!

Showing is a pursuit which keeps the family together; often father drives the box and mother supervises the catering – in other words, is chief cook and bottle-washer – whilst the other members of the family have their own duties with the horses and ponies. It was with this in mind that the BSPS introduced intermediate classes so that the older members of the family (up to 25 years of age) could compete alongside their younger brothers and sisters at the same show. However, a word of warning: there are few places these days where children can be left by parents knowing that they will be safe from the more unpleasant aspects of life and although a showfield is usually very safe, it is not totally devoid of crime: so keep an eye on children, and keep valuables under lock and key.

Some stalwarts of the showing world feel that there are very few individual stars in the ring today compared to the past, just as many also feel that the friendliness has gone, especially at shows like Wembley. But in my opinion it is the growth of the activity which gives rise to such statements. The pony classes, for instance, are of a higher general standard today and as a result it is difficult to make a star of an individual – in the past, after the two or three at the top the class would tail-off badly. Similarly, the friendliness is certainly still there, but due to the vast number of people involved it is increasingly difficult to know everyone – inevitably one often feels surrounded by strangers. And the formation of areas in the BSPS has naturally meant that people tend to make friends from their own little group, whether this is based on the type of class they compete in or on their geographical area.

In the past there were basically only three main winter functions: a dance at Oakham organised by Dorothy Watchorn, one at Barnby Moor organised by Joy Massarella and the Welsh dance at the Green Dragon organised by Mr and Mrs Eckley. These days however, there is more social activity within each area, which does result in fewer people mixing on a nationwide scale; and furthermore the current trend is for many new people to come into the game: some stop with us forever, others leave as quickly as they come, maybe taking a major prize with them on the way. From an overall and business point of view this is not a bad state of affairs, since it ensures that showing will be a continuous process and not a thing of the past. With this in mind, many showing societies, though unfortunately not all, are making extensive moves to keep showing up to a modern-day standard, and are looking ahead to a bright future.

CHAPTER 2

Finding your Champion

So you have decided to enter the world of showing – in that case you will need a suitable animal. If you are lucky enough to find perfection on four legs, many hours of pleasure will be enjoyed. However, the wrong animal may put you off altogether, so a lot of time and effort must be spent in pursuit of the right one.

THE RIGHT CHOICE

Buying a horse or pony is not like buying a dog: for example, it does not share your home, but requires a stable and field of its own – this is a basic necessity; moreover the horse is more complicated to deal with, and also needs an expensive wardrobe. Some people are under the impression that buying a horse or pony is like buying a car, but although the initial purchase may be similar, the show animal is not a machine which can be turned on and off at the flick of a switch. This animal has an independent mind very much like that of a spoilt child, and likewise requires the necessary attention. The introduction of a show animal to a family has more often than not completely changed the life of everyone.

Before looking at a prospective purchase, be sure in your own mind as to the sort of animal you require; it may be a good idea to travel to a few shows to see the sort of standard expected and also which possibilities might be open to you. How heavily are you going to become involved? Are you, like most people, going to feel your way by competing initially at Riding Club shows, or are you going to compete at top level showing straightaway? In the north there are several 'levels' of showing so you can cut your suit according to your cloth. An age-old piece of advice given to my father by an old horsemaster in the early days, was that it costs the same to keep a good 'un as a bad 'un, and that there was more chance of winning with the former and therefore getting a return on your money; although it must be said that if an animal is doing a specific job, you should be prepared for it to lose some of its value, just as a car will depreciate in value.

Buying a Champion

Remember that if you buy a champion, it may have to be produced and ridden by people more competent than yourself, and then the total expense of the venture and the consequent pressure may detract somewhat from the fun element. However, it is understandable that people successful in life like to buy the best they can afford, and sometimes money is of no object – this sort of person usually thrives on success and does not like to take a back seat even when competing at 'hobby' level. Equally there are those other people whose success has often come from making good from nothing, and who like to find new talent – it is this which gives them a sense of achievement, they do not want to follow someone else's success and often believe that if you buy at the top end of the market you may be buying a name rather than a product, and paying well over the animal's true value for the privilege.

In fact when an animal is at the top, there is only one way for it to go eventually, and it is often far more fun to ride along on a wave of success which takes you from obscurity to dizzy heights, than it is to fight off the heir apparents who are trying to topple you from your throne. In short, it is much easier and more rewarding to take an unknown animal to the top than to keep a former champion at the top for a long period. So the best advice, once you have a clear idea of your aim, is to get the best possible animal for the price which you can afford and mount your child or yourself on the best that is available at the time.

Shop Around

Equines are not like other commodities; unlike a car, where a particular model and vintage is a similar price from garage to garage, a horse is worth whatever a buyer is willing to spend, so it does pay to shop around. This does not mean that you should mess people about, and have weekend holidays at other people's expense; most vendors go to a lot of trouble to present an animal to a prospective buyer and can usually tell from the conversation if the purchaser is the genuine article – you may become labelled a time-waster.

It is very difficult to find anything top class these days and very rarely do you find what you want; if you do discover a high class animal on your travels, even if it is not the type you originally wanted it pays to keep an open mind and seriously consider it. We have often bought, for example, a riding horse when actually looking for a show hunter pony.

I was once told a story about a certain professional who was winning on something which was high class, but not really top class; the rider of the second horse said 'Well, you've gone down in my estimation sitting on something like that.' To which the professional replied, 'We are all looking for the ideal, but unfortunately this only comes along once in a blue moon – why should I spend my showing career in semi-retirement in the meantime when I can be seen winning on this?'

This is very true, especially as the standard of competition in some years can vary quite remarkably in some classes, and a mediocre animal if it is well produced may well be accepted by the judges. On the other hand, you can soon lose credibility in the eyes of the judge if you are seen too often with an 'also-ran' at the bigger shows. Basically it is the responsibility of both judge and exhibitor to maintain and improve standards.

Suitability

When looking for show animals another major point to consider is, how capable are the people who will have to take charge of the animal, not only at home but also in the ring? At home, the job is difficult enough without taking on any extra problems – although there are those who see problems as a challenge and would view the most placid, wonderfully tempered hack as a positive bore. If it is a family set-up with a lot of young people around, it is better to be safe than sorry. For example, it is no use a small, feeble handler attempting to show a big strapping three-year-old hunter or an over-exuberant Arab stallion.

When purchasing a ridden exhibit, it is important to match the horse or pony with the rider. This observation is particularly important for someone making the transition from ponies to horses; I was fortunate to have the lightweight hunter Portman Lad, who could do weight classes, riding horse and working hunter classes and had also won at the RIHS side-saddle with his previous owner Mrs Janet Cope. It is also important when very small children are concerned, especially when they are going solo in their first ridden classes. It is only common sense not to put a novice rider on a novice animal – the theory that both will learn together is nonsense.

A top class champion may not be the best bet either, and one often sees a former winner going badly because it has learned to take advantage of a less capable jockey – you would not, for example, allow a learner driver to jump into a high-powered sports car.

The Schoolmaster

Just as a genuine grade A horse will teach the novice show jumping rider all about strides and so on, so a schoolmaster show animal will be a blessing to a nervous novice rider. Every successful rider has at some point in his riding career benefited from a seasoned animal; the schoolmaster may be just getting past his best, but he is there to do another job and jockeys will come on in leaps and bounds, gaining confidence and able to learn more if they do not have to worry whether the animal is going to spook or go on the wrong leg. A schoolmaster which can still win at top level shows is definitely worth its weight in gold. Not all evergreen horses and ponies are Christians though; some will have picked up many tricks and can be very ring crafty, especially some of the ridden hunters which are always ready to gallop after two circuits of the ring at canter.

Novices and In-hand

Some novice ponies on the other hand will only pick up what they are taught, and more often than not need a jockey with experience to give them the security to improve. How often do you see the big in-hand winner go to a novice showing home never to be seen again, simply because the breeder has been offered a lot of money? Although in the short term he has benefited, in the long term, unless the animal is successful, that stud will slip into obscurity. It is better policy for a breeder to give his animal the best possible chance and take the home into consideration, especially if there are brothers and sisters from that line waiting in the wings. People are always asking, why do we not see more in-hand winners under saddle? And this could be one reason.

Breeders

Breeders are generally at a disadvantage compared to the everyday buyer; as the late Mr Joe Massarella said 'You breed what God gives you, but you can buy whatever you want.' If you feel that you are incapable of choosing a good animal on your own and need advice, go to a knowledgeable person like a professional, who has his finger on the pulse of the showing world. As long as you do not mind paying for the advice, you are probably better off in his capable hands. Most of the time these people will put you on the right track, valuing your custom.

It pays to remember that some ponies which have become institutionalised in a professional yard will take advantage of a more low-key set-up. Similarly, there are others which will benefit from the more individual attention a family home can provide – some of the stars do thrive on this personal service. Amateurs do put themselves down unnecessarily at times and in my opinion are often underestimated. It is often when animals change hands that the tide of fortune can also alter.

Mare or Gelding?

Another consideration is whether you prefer a mare or a gelding; a stallion must never be handled by a complete novice. Some people get on better with mares, and of course these can be bred from afterwards, which gives them another job in later life; geldings can either be retired at the top or must gradually slip down the rungs of the ladder – and there is nothing more distressing than seeing a past big winner looking and going a shadow of its former self at some tatty little show. Personally, I have always found the geldings more straightforward and if they need a 'squaring-up' they don't usually sulk afterwards like mares.

To summarise: when choosing a pony take into account:

a The price you can afford – although the buying is not always the problem, but the cost afterwards.

b The ability of the people involved with the production and presentation.

c The facilities and amount of time available.

CONFORMATION

The perfect animal has not been bred: even the outstanding champion has a chink in the china, so we must be content with looking for near perfection instead. Good conformation, whether it be in a lead-rein pony or a heavyweight cob, is not only pleasing to the eye, it also has a more practical function. If the ridden animal is put together correctly, he should give a comfortable ride and he will be more efficient in the way he goes, therefore putting less stress and strain on his structure.

For instance, if a horse has a twisted near foreleg there will be more strain on this leg, than on the off foreleg which stands true. If a pony is thick through the jowl it will have difficulty in flexing, giving an unbalanced ride, which will probably also lead to respiratory problems later on. A good, sloping shoulder will give a good flowing ride, whilst a horse with an upright shoulder often

When looking at a horse, always stand back to assess the overall picture

accompanied by a flat wither will give a very downhill, jarring ride, putting wear on the limbs. There are some slight exceptions to the rule, however; pasterns should be short, although slightly long pasterns, despite being weaker, do give the ride more spring; this is not to be confused with upright pasterns which give a choppy ride and are not ideal. Similarly a long back, although a weakness, usually gives a comfortable ride as you are sitting in the middle; with a short-coupled animal it can feel as if you are being thrown out of the saddle, because you are sitting on the roof of the boiler room so to speak – besides which these animals are more prone to overreaching.

It is interesting to note that it is usually the good horsemen rather than the show pony people who are more aware of correctness of conformation, knowing which problems can occur as a direct result of structural faults.

When looking at a horse, always stand back to assess the overall picture: this should be one of balance and proportion. You will then be able to see if it is higher behind than in front (this will alter in young, late-maturing animals) which usually gives a downhill ride, or whether its body is too big for its limbs. Ideally you are looking for a topline which should be a series of scenic curves from the poll to the tail.

The Forehand

Everybody likes to see a show animal with an attractive head; however, if it is slightly plain, better this than a bad hind leg, because a clever producer can cover up a head with a thicker bridle but he can do little to cover up a bad hind leg. A head which is too large for its body will result in the animal falling on its forehand and being heavy in the rider's hand. And I do like to see a well-defined eye; the eye has been described as the mirror of the soul, and a small piggy one usually denotes a meanness of character.

The neck should be well set on and form a well-defined arch – a convex topline – from the withers to the poll. Most judges look for a good fronted animal; there is nothing worse than the feeling a poor front gives you, as if you were sitting on the edge of a cliff – as Mrs Norman Crow says, 'A good front keeps you on board if you meet a drop fence.' A good front is one which has a decent length of rein, and this includes a nicely sloping shoulder, not just a long neck with an upright shoulder. Horses with ewe necks (upside-down, or a concave topline) often give a strong, unbalanced ride.

Back and Quarters

A horse that is narrow to sit on (the razorblade type) is often uncomfortable and a poor doer; whereas a horse that is too broad in the chest (the barmaid look!) and barrelly (sprung-ribbed) will tend to give a rolling feeling in canter and gallop. The ridden horse should have a deep girth line; this denotes plenty of heart room and prevents the saddle from slipping forward. The back must be strong to carry the weight of the saddle and rider. A hollow back, usually a sign of old age, is a definite weakness – although a leading show hack from a few years ago had this fault and gave the judges a wonderful ride; a rider was slotted into the geography of the horse, so to speak, rather like a clothes peg on a line. A roach, or hog back is the opposite and although a lot stronger it usually gives a very rough, bumpy ride.

The hindquarters are the engine-room, and I do like to see a big, well-muscled area with a good length of croup which is in proportion to the rest of the body, and particularly a strong second thigh. From behind it should be a picture of squareness and symmetry.

Limbs

Limbs should be well-defined and flint-like, showing no signs of either puffiness or wear and tear. The forearm takes the strain of the horse's weight and should be well formed and straight from the elbow to the pastern. The knee should be clean (not broken, which means the skin has been broken), broad and flat. If an animal is 'over at the knee' this is not a particular fault; racing people in fact almost prefer this as they say it saves the tendons at the back of the foreleg, so there is less chance of breaking down. However, forelegs which are 'back at the knee' are a major fault in a show ring; this is typical of commoner breeds and can be seen in some of today's show cobs with draught breeding. The cannon bone is equivalent to the human middle finger from wrist to knuckle and should be short and strong. The larger the circumference of bone below the knee, the greater the weight-carrying capacity of the horse. In the show ring, however, some judges would rather see quality bone, even though there may be less of it, than a lot of more common bone – hence the saying, 'An ounce of blood is worth an inch of bone': Thoroughbred bone is quality bone and has a greater strength and density than the bone of commoner breeds.

If the foreleg is narrower just below the knee it is called 'tied in below the knee'; similarly, if the circumference just below the hock is less than lower down the leg, it is called 'light of bone below the hock' – both are faults and undesirable. The fetlock joint is the shock absorber and should be broad and flat; it should not be filled – such a horse is said to be 'round of its joints' – which is usually a sign that the animal has had a lot of hard work.

Hindlegs

If the hindquarters are the engine-room, the hindleg is the engine and the source of propulsion (*ie* the hock joint and second thigh). It should follow a vertical line from the point of the buttock, over the point of the hock down the back of the tendons to the ground. Sickle hocks occur when the angle of each hock is too acute, so they form a sickle shape; the more severe the angle, the greater the weakness. Straight hocks are the opposite and result in a rather short, shuffly stride which puts a strain on the joints. Viewed from the back, neither cow hocks (hocks turned in) nor bow hocks (hocks turned out) are acceptable in a top-class show ring.

The Foot
The foot is probably the most important feature of any horse – what is the use of having the most perfect-looking animal if it has four bad feet? The angle of the front foot should be approximately forty-five degrees; the hind foot, sixty degrees. A fault seen all too often in the ring today is that of the toe being too long and the heel too severely trimmed; or the toes have been dumped – trimmed off short – usually to fit the shoe. An animal should stand four square on all his feet, toes turning neither in nor out, and the front and hind feet should be two matched pairs, the hind feet being slightly more upright and narrower. Small feet are bad, especially in deep going, and over-large feet can make the animal look clumsy; boxy, upright feet are not accepted in the show ring. Judges should be able to distinguish between laminitis rings (as a result of laminitis), and grass rings which appear after a long period at grass. The frog should always be kept clean and healthy, as this is the shock-absorbing part of the foot.

Movement
Natural movement is a gift from the gods and every trainer's dream. If an animal has a bad trot it is up to the trainer to decide at which speed it camouflages this fault best. Usually, if an animal walks well it is said to have a good canter and gallop (top gear). Movement is related to conformation; if an animal stands true, it should in theory move straight – horses narrow in front often plait (cross one foot in front of the other in movement) and 'bosomy' ones often dish (throw the front feet out). Cow hocks usually lead to horses moving close behind; out-turned hocks produce wide movement behind – hence the saying 'you could get a bus through those back legs'. If an animal is 'tied in at the elbow' he will only move from here, and will give only the appearance of pointing his toe; similarly a horse with an upright shoulder (as opposed to a good sloping one) will have a short stride. Over-straight hocks, and hocks 'in the air' both usually make hock engagement that much more difficult; however, over-

bent hocks (sickle), even though they may be unsightly and frowned upon in the ring, do exaggerate the idea of the hocks being well underneath the animal and therefore creating impulsion. In racing circles it is often said that a horse with a sickle hock will be able to gallop well.

Lumps and Bumps

As well as faults of conformation, a judge must take into consideration lumps and bumps. If two animals are exactly equal, then the clean-limbed animal must get the decision. Not all bumps are directly linked to an animal's defects in conformation; some are manmade through too much work or a strain, sometimes even a knock in the field. A splint is a blemish, but depending on where it is and how unsightly, you can at times overlook it. However, a curb is a sign of weakness as well as unsoundness, and must be heavily penalised. Bog spavin, bone spavin and thoroughpin are usually found in weak hocks and are also unsoundnesses.

Extra Essentials

When judging, whether it be in-hand or under saddle, I always like to see an animal with scope. This means he should stand over a lot of ground yet still be in proportion – not to be confused with something which is long in the back (known as the 'family animal' – all the family can sit on it at the same time!). A lot of people use the word quality without thinking how they would interpret it, and most have a slightly different definition; but it is simply something good, of extra refinement and class (as opposed to coarseness) which pleases the eye. Very closely connected with this is the term presence, which must not be mistaken for something flashy or over-exuberant: presence is that extra something which makes you look at an animal again and again. The standard of competition is so great nowadays that it is much harder to achieve success with animals which are lacking in these essential extras.

TYPES

Judging is based on opinion and what pleases the judge on the day; however, just as with conformation, there are certain ground rules as to type in the same way that there are breed characteristics in mountain and moorland, and Arab classes.

Hunters

The show hunter is the near perfect model of the horse in the hunting field, with plenty of quality. Ideally a Thoroughbred with a good temperament, he must be sound and stand on the best of legs, and his body must be of hunter type and suitable for heart and lungs to work efficiently whilst performing. There are three main weight categories, although at small shows these are sometimes amalgamated, and each weight category is determined above all by the amount of bone below the knee. The lightweight hunter should have approximately 8½in of bone (remember some of our native ponies have 8in (20cm)) and be capable of carrying no more than 12st 7lb (80kg). This class usually contains a very high class Thoroughbred type of horse which gallops well and gives a very light, accurate ride. The judges must try and stick to the right type, unless circumstances make the task impossible – for instance, if a horse has gone so well and is difficult to fault in relation to the other contenders.

The middleweight horse, like the 13.2hh show pony, is usually the true pattern for the section it represents and often wins championships. He should be capable of carrying 12st 7lb – 14st (80–90kg), and have 8½–9in of bone. He can be bolder in his ride and even though some of the horses that win lack the quality of the lightweight, this is something the true champion never lacks. It is said that when the quality horse gallops, there will scarcely be a tremor as he thunders past the grandstand, whereas the under-bred horse will shake the ground like an earthquake.

The heavyweight hunter must be capable of carrying over 14st (90kg) and have at least 9in of bone; this category can be a real mixed bag and some of the exhibits are really lumbering, common specimens which have been cleverly produced. The quality heavyweight show horse is a rarity indeed: he is not required to, and usually does not move at trot in as spectacular a fashion as the lightweight, nor is he as speedy at the gallop; but he fills the eye in majestic supremacy.

In novice, ladies and working classes the weight classifications are not as important. A certain amount of greenness is accepted in the novices, especially in the four-year-old classes; and in the ladies, a smaller, lighter type of hunter can win – the priorities here are a smooth, well balanced, unexaggerated ride, a good front and exceptional manners.

The small hunter class has produced some outstanding types, and of all the hunter classes, this is the ideal for younger riders; at one time it was called the juvenile hunter class. Ideally the small

*The quality heavyweight show hunter is a rarity indeed –
Seabrook, Show Hunter of the Year, 1984, 1986 and 1987*

*A perfect ladies' hunter must give a smooth, well-balanced,
unexaggerated ride, and have a good front and exceptional
manners*

Statesman, Small Hunter of the Year in 1979 and 1983, and Overall Hunter Champion at the Royal International Horse Show, 1985

hunter should be more of a middleweight than a lightweight, full of quality but deep and butty on a short leg. It is a great pity that this representative is not allowed in championships more often.

Hacks
The show hack or park hack (as opposed to the covert hack) is a product of Edwardian and Victorian social life, and can best be summed up in three words: grace, elegance and manners. Hacks

are not a breed as such, but are instead discovered. Jack Hance described them as 'fine weather birds', and in the words of Count Robert Orssich they should be 'a pleasure to ride, not a penance'. Just as a hunter should be workmanlike and correct, the hack should be a thing of beauty and correctness. Again, it should ideally be a Thoroughbred, although today there is a mixture of Arab types, pony types and small hunter types – in fact the true hack types could be named on one hand. Hopefully the new hack breeding classes which the BSHC&RHA has put under its wing, will do something constructive to counteract this. The hack is shown in two categories: small, which is up to 15hh, and large, 15hh to 15.3hh. He should walk into the ring with unlimited, mannerly exuberance; his action should be light and spectacular at trot, and his canter collected and smooth with the hocks well underneath. He must be a pleasure to watch and a pleasure to ride.

Cobs

The cob is a type described by his name alone: up to 15.1hh, he should be compact, short-legged and have the bone and substance of a heavyweight hunter. He must be well mannered and well schooled, with a view to being ridden by an elderly gentleman. A cob should have a noble head, a generous eye, a shapely neck with a cresty top line and a hogged mane, well defined withers, plenty of depth and clean strong hocks; he is also expected to gallop, although not with the elastic stride of a hunter. There are many classes for the cob: novice, working, amateur/owner as well as the two weight classes – lightweights carry up to 14st (90kg) and have at least 8½in of bone; and the heavyweight has at least 9in of bone and is capable of carrying a rider over 14st. The popularity of this show animal has increased beyond belief, largely due to the hard work of Muriel Bowen, who in ten years has raised over £91,000 in sponsorship for cob classes. In the ring today, however, one often sees weight-carrying cobs which masquerade as show cobs; these are really vanners, characterised by the common head, the high harness action and common round limbs – and a ride like a bone-shaker!

Riding Horses

The riding horse classes are one of the recent success stories of the BSHC&RHA and are slowly taking over in popularity from the hack classes – just as the WHP classes are superseding the show ponies. This does not mean to say that the hacks and show ponies are going to die a death, they will always be there.

Grandstand, Cob of the Year, 1982–4 and 1986

Roy Trigg on Johnathon, Cob of the Year, 1969, 1970,
1972 and 1973 (Monty)

The ultimate achievement: Burroprince, Riding Horse of
the Year, 1987 and 1988, under the spotlight

Small riding horse J.C.B., Champion at the Royal International Horse Show in 1988 and 1989

The society recommends that a riding horse should have quality, substance, good bone, correct conformation, presence and true action. Something between a hack and a hunter, while not requiring the substance of the latter or the elegance of the former, it should be up to sufficient weight to carry an average adult and at the same time be a comfortable ride and show an ability to gallop.

The small riding horse is up to 15.2hh, and therefore copes with a height range which size for size suits the average adult rider. The large riding horse is over 15.2hh, and gives many owners the chance to show a good, well schooled horse which would otherwise not have a class to enter. When judging, the emphasis is on manners, ride and training.

Ponies

Our show ponies are the envy of the world – I can still recall the disbelief on the faces of some German visitors when watching the ponies awaiting the championship in the Wembley collecting ring. The pony classes still attract the biggest crowds during Wembley week. Since the development of the working hunter pony (WHP) and show hunter pony (SHP) classes, the true show pony type has been strengthened; the best way to differentiate between the two is to imagine them 'blown up' to horse size – the show pony will look like a hack, and the WHP/SHP a hunter. As opinions differ, some judges still go for the miniature riding horses in both sections.

Astronomical prices are paid for show ponies, far more than for their horse counterparts, simply because children are involved and most parents want the best for their offspring whilst they are still within a particular age group. I believe this is also the reason why there is so much back-biting in the pony scene – parents try much too hard on behalf of their children. When we went up to horse classes, the hunter people used to label us as 'pony people' and were very wary of us, I can tell you!

Leading Rein
The leading rein classes are a delight to watch, and the trick to this class is to create the right picture. It is therefore just as important to find the right pony to suit the child (especially as this is usually the family's first good pony anyway) as it is to find the right colour combinations of ties, ribbons and browbands. There are two height categories at the BSPS Championships and at the bigger shows: up to 11.2hh, and from 11.2hh to 12hh – this allows for jockeys growing. It is important that you don't put a very weeny jockey on an up-to-height pony as this will create an unbalanced picture (like you see in the Thelwell books). It goes without saying that with such small children manners are of paramount importance, and if a pony shakes its head or stops suddenly or even breaks into an unsolicited canter, it could go plummeting down the line. You want to see a relaxed, dainty movement – not too long a stride, or the jockey will be thumping up and down like a beach ball; and obedience to the jockey's riding ability is essential. The handler is merely the safety cord; I myself do like to see the more competent jockeys in more control than the little dots who are merely passengers. There are predominantly two distinct pony types: the characteristic Welsh

31

which can still hold their own under certain judges; and the more blood pony type which, providing they don't behave like miniature racehorses, do gain a fair share of the spoils.

First Ridden

The first ridden class is one of the most important stages in a jockey's riding career – showing as an individual, with no handler as a safety net. If a jockey becomes frightened at this stage it is very difficult to get that all-important confidence back. Some ponies do both lead rein and first ridden classes, although ponies which are angelic on the lead rein can be real horrors as solo mounts. The first ridden pony can be scopier in shape and slightly bolder in its way of going – it should go freely forward with good smooth transitions; it will be expected to canter in its individual show with the jockey in complete control, so again, manners are very important. The individual shows will usually sort out a class and can result in the final placings being quite different from the initial pull-in.

Height Classes

There are three open classes, and the 12.2hh for riders up to twelve years old caters for the smallest. Although the miniature blood type ponies tend to dominate this class, the more quality native pony can also hold his own. A more sophisticated way of going is expected than for the first ridden.

The 13.2hh class with riders up to fourteen years of age, is the height group which should provide the champion, the true open pony with quality, good movement and the ability to use all the gears in all the paces.

The 14.2hh class is a particular favourite as the jockeys (up to sixteen years old) ride like mini-professionals and can get the very best out of the ponies – in this class we see ponies going for their lives, and it is often this showmanship which makes the champion. Because the jockeys are expected to be more competent, high spirits (rather than bad manners) will be overlooked by some judges. Watching this class category is particularly interesting because you can usually understand a judge's placings, especially in type – whether he goes for the 14hh pony sort, which for some would lack scope; or whether he prefers the bigger-

Langfield Harvest Time, 12.2hh Pony of the Year, 1987, and Champion at the Royal International Horse Show, 1988

made pony, up-to-height but which may be a bit horsey for some. This is certainly not the class for the cowardly or slow-thinking jockey.

Novice

In novice classes you obviously judge a performance on the day, but if there are ponies very close to each other in pattern and performance, I believe that you should give the first prize to the one which you think will have the most potential to make it in the big time. Unfortunately too many novice ponies are already at their best at this stage and will not have the scope or the guts/charm to develop any further; their careers are therefore very short-lived. The old method of having to watch the closing date for entries was hard work and you had to be a genius to make sure that you got the maximum number of novice classes in the showing season. We used to de-novice ponies over the spring bank holiday and this enabled us to show the novices as late as the East of England and Royal Welsh shows. However, with the present-day methods, you can stay a novice all season unless you win an open class or open championship, and this does give the owner more control and say in his pony's novice career. Even though three-year-old ponies can be shown under saddle after July, I personally do not like to see this. Too many ponies do not reach their full potential under saddle because their production is rushed, and this is one particular area which emphasises this point – although I might add it didn't damage Holly of Spring, who was Novice BSPS champion at three years old.

Juvenile and Intermediate

The juvenile class will hopefully establish a more definite type now that the intermediate classes have been launched; at present it is for horses up to 15hh and exceeding 14hh, and for riders not to have attained their eighteenth birthday before 1 January in the current year. In this class we are still looking for some pony characteristics; we don't want a show hunter pony and the horsey type will be better catered for in the new intermediate classes – in my opinion this is a class for the pony type hack which is so often seen in the small hack class. I would not be particularly looking for an extension of a 14.2hh pony, I prefer possibly a bit more substance than that; but it is important that it should retain its pony characteristics.

There has been much criticism hurled at the new intermediate classes, mostly by breeders who think that putting on 15.2hh classes for the older BSPS members is a step towards losing 'pony thinking'. However, a great many members *have* felt differently and they must be accommodated, their feeling being that not all teenagers are either lucky enough, or sufficiently mature, to go straight into the deep end with adult professionals. Time will tell, but I think it is a great pity that the horse societies could not accommodate this age group (16–25) instead. If these, and the juvenile classes, are in theory giving the young adult a chance to develop albeit in a more welcoming environment, it is nonetheless important that judges ask more from them in standard of training as a part of their education.

Show Hunter and Working Hunter Pony (SHP & WHP)

The show hunter pony classes (like the riding horse classes) are as successful as were the WHP classes when they were started all those years ago. The children seem to enjoy competing in these, which is more than can be said for the show pony classes. There are basically four categories: 12hh, 13hh, 14hh and 15hh, and these should be miniature versions of the show hunter classes. I prefer the middleweight/heavyweight types; this often surprises exhibitors who think that because I produce show ponies, I am more likely to lean towards fineness. Above all, the hunter pony should be a definite stamp, with good limbs and an ability to gallop – some judges don't even ask for a figure-of-eight because they would rather see a good lengthening of stride. The standard of these classes is increasing all the time, and there is now a distinct difference between a typical SHP and a WHP – just as there is in the Hunter Improvement Society (HIS) classes. Perhaps one of the hardest classes to judge is the 12hh class, as those contending it are usually such a mixed bunch of all shapes and sizes. Of the 15hh class, my only criticism is that some are bordering on being too horsey. But the pleasing thing is that these classes give the competent child two classes to compete in (SHP and WHP); and if for some reason a fabulous-looking WHP will not jump, it means that he now has a class to enter instead of being made redundant.

THE FINAL DECISION: BUYING

Having at last decided on the type of horse or pony you want, you may find that attending shows will help you make your final choice. Very rarely is the showground the best place actually to try the animal – you don't want people to know all your business,

and in fact some vendors won't allow this at all. However, there are exceptions – for instance the Peterborough championships are a good meeting place for people from all ends of the country. So if someone from Scotland is interested in an animal from Surrey it makes more sense economically to see it at Peterborough since the rider and lorry will be there anyway. And since a veterinary surgeon will also be there, this will save any extra expense incurred by his travelling costs.

Under normal circumstances, people will try a pony or horse at the stables at which it is kept. Arrange a time to arrive there – always make an appointment, even if it is a spur-of-the-moment decision because you will be passing the end of the road or have a free Sunday afternoon. Try to be punctual, although weather and traffic conditions can put paid to this! Nor should you try to get there early in the hope of seeing if the animal is being heavily worked-in – it is just as rude to arrive too early as it is too late. If we have made good time, we often stop somewhere for a cup of coffee, or ring the people to ask if we might call slightly earlier.

On arrival at the yard, do remember you have come to look at a pony, and not to take a look around everything else – a stable yard is like another room in the house and should be treated as such. Always see the pony in the box first, then see it outside to assess its conformation; ask for it to be walked and trotted in-hand. If at any stage you definitely do not like the pony, say something, rather than waste everybody's time. Although some owners may take offence and be insulted, I always try to say what I think, as it is only fair in the long run – any ill-feeling is usually caused not by what you actually say, but the way in which you say it, in a situation like this. Remember, if you are buying a ridden pony, some animals may look better when under saddle; so if you are keeping an open mind, let the procedure continue. Often the owner himself, or his groom or child will work the animal in first, and your jockey can ride it afterwards. It is so difficult, even for the expert, to be able to assess an animal in the short time given – judges are expected to do it, but not to then buy the animal on the basis of their own judgement. However, it is better to use this one opportunity to be really sure of an animal, rather than keep going back week after week – it is so easy to become labelled a timewaster.

If you try the animal in a confined space like an outdoor or indoor arena, ask if it is also possible to try it in a field so you can

Runnings Park Brut, Champion Show Hunter Pony at the RIHS, 1987

gauge its reaction in the open; we often allow the prospective purchaser to hack the animal out, in company of course. Always remember that you are there as a prospective buyer, and therefore do not abuse your position by overworking or overexerting the animal. If at the end of the day you are still not sure, you can always ask if you might take the animal on a week's trial – if the vendor has seen that you have treated the animal with respect, an arrangement could be made.

If a deal has been struck and a reasonable amount of money is to change hands, it is always more sensible to arrange a vetting. Some people allow gut feeling and their own judgement to guide them, but even if everything on the surface looks acceptable, there may be something else wrong which only a vet could detect. After all, if you work hard on the animal and then wish to sell it on again to a private person, imagine how disappointed you will be if it is spun by the vet.

If you have not taken a measuring stick with you, it is always wise to ask your vet to measure the animal if height is important for your purposes, even if it possesses a life height certificate. If the animal is passed by the vet and you have made a deal to buy it 'subject to vet' – it is now your animal in principal. Don't take too long in collecting it; technically the vendors could charge you livery, as from the day you rang to let them know that everything was well.

The Latin 'Caveat Emptor' very much applies: it is up to you as a purchaser to ask all the relevant questions – there aren't many vendors who will admit every little defect, in case they should put a buyer off. Someone once said 'if you are old enough to have a cheque book, you are old enough to go out and buy, and if something does not turn out as you had planned, then put it down to experience.' One way to learn, however hard, is through your pocket! However, with all the legal complications these days, it is wise for any vendor to be honest and helpful, as a satisfied customer will always return; and if you have any respect for your animal you will try and accommodate him in the right home.

CHAPTER 3

Running a Show Yard

One of the most important aspects of a showing yard is the atmosphere; it must be relaxed and interesting, not only from the human point of view but also for the show animals. There must be a good balance of peace and quiet, yet enough activity for the stock to view to prevent them getting bored, as boredom may lead to vices such as windsucking and weaving.

One of the nicest showing yards is 'Little Barn', which belongs to Miss Stella Harries; it is like a model village and the inmates can see plenty of activity, as horses and people go in and out of the indoor school and visitors call at the house. Not all the stables look into the fields, however, and this is not a bad idea as some stabled horses become upset when they see their friends frolicking about outside.

My yard is three-sided, so the animals are able to study the activity within the yard and can look across the fields on the fourth side. The yard was built in a field to the left of the house and so there are a lot of birds in the surrounding trees and hedges, and these in turn contribute to the sedate atmosphere. I recall seeing Gem's Signet at Mrs McMullen's yard in Norfolk the first year he was shown under saddle and particularly remember how peaceful the yard was, and this is an important consideration, as show animals need to be able to wind down after a busy show.

YARD LAYOUT

If you are building a yard from scratch, plan it carefully; we were fortunate to have the help of Brenda Legge who had worked in a few different yards and made a very practical contribution to the planning. The first essential is to have every facility within easy reach, as so much time can be wasted walking about unnecessarily. One of the major activities is mucking out and bedding down, so it is sensible to have both the muck heap and hay/straw store near to hand – those bales get heavier after the first one, not lighter! Both should also be accessible for lorries so that the muck heap may be cleared away with ease, and when hay, straw or food is delivered, carrying is kept to a minimum.

The feedroom is the focal point of the yard and is best located at a central point; if buckets have to be carried a long distance, feeding can take a long time. The trouble is, if it is in the middle of the yard the greedier animals are impatient at feed times and kick at the doors when they see people in the feedroom. In ours we have a sink with hot and cold water and also a cooker, so that it doubles as a utility room.

Tackroom

For security reasons our tackroom is nearer the house than the yard – which causes problems if you have almost tacked up and have forgotten something like a girth and have to go back for it! Having an organised tackroom is very important because it is a work-room when cleaning tack, and also a storage room for rugs and so on. With this in mind, having some sort of heating system is vital to prevent the contents becoming damp and mouldy. We have a large saddle-horse in the centre of the room to make cleaning easier (rather than against a wall). There can never be too many saddle racks and bridle hooks in a tackroom – these can be expensive, so for the latter we use small dog-food tins nailed to the wall. The saddle-horse came from the sales, as did some of the blanket boxes and old wardrobes which are very useful for storing things. Some tackrooms have a carpet on the floor which I consider very impractical – it is so easy to knock a bucket of water over by accident.

Whether the focal point of the yard is the feedroom or the tackroom, it is important that a list of a few main telephone numbers is left in there, just in case there is an emergency when the house is locked up. We used to have a telephone in the tackroom and then the feedroom, but now we have a cordless one which we can use even in the fields or outdoor school. Whilst on the subject of emergencies: it is always advisable to have an isolation stable just in case an animal starts, for example, coughing – some illnesses can spread like wildfire through a yard and halt all showing activity within a week.

Ground Surface

What often makes a good yard and gives it the final polish is the surface – we have concrete around the front of the boxes – and this extends beyond the width of the stable overhang – and gravel in the middle. People often ask us why we didn't concrete the whole yard; the reason is that not only would it have looked a little stark, but on a windy day nothing is more soul-destroying than having to sweep a concrete yard full of debris. We sweep the loose hay and straw onto the gravel and then rake it up, which is a lot easier! Also on a very frosty morning, concrete can be very slippery – just as tarmac roads are in summer. Anything which makes the surroundings and working environment more pleasant, even in a big busy yard, and helps to create a happy yard is worth the extra effort. We have an ornamental well in the middle of the gravel which is overflowing with flowers during the show season, and also numerous hanging baskets which some of the ponies devour!

However, no matter how much effort is made to give a place extra charm, you must never lose sight of practicality. For example, it is essential to have a well-drained working area for washing down horses in preparation for shows, or for hosing down legs if injured etc. There is nothing worse than going into a yard which has mud and water collecting in it because of insufficient or inadequate drainage.

One piece of construction which was more ornamental than practical at the time of planning, but which has since proved to be essential in the day-to-day running of the yard, has been the archway leading to the outdoor school and fields. It has doubled as a hay store, measuring pad, a bathing area when it has been chilly or when all the other boxes have been occupied, but most importantly it has helped enormously with bad loaders. If you drop the ramp down within the tunnel the animal can only go forwards, or backwards onto your threatening broom, and up to now this method has proved 100% successful.

Gates

Gates are vital. At Blue Slate there is the archway entrance and another wider gateway into the yard – the farrier uses this so that he can work in the stables area from the back of his car. Both of these have gates on them – it is essential that a stable yard is gated so that animals cannot escape; some of our show ponies are real Houdinis! We also have gates to all the fields, and the outdoor school – better to be safe than sorry.

FENCING AND FIELDS

All the fields are fenced with posts and rails which are creosoted regularly to prevent the ponies from chewing them. Even though some owners still use wire, saying that stock respect it, I have seen some horrific accidents when animals have been caught in it.

Even if your show animal is only out in the fields for a couple of hours during the show season, a fresh supply of water should always be available along with some form of field shelter so that he can escape from the flies. Both of these are essential if ponies are turned away on a more permanent basis, as in winter. A useful idea, especially if you have only one water trough, is to make a gated cattle-pen so that whichever field you use, the water trough can always be reached. This would also double as a catch-pen in the event of a horse or pony being difficult to catch. If you need to use both fields simultaneously include the water tank in the fencing.

THE ALL-WEATHER MANÈGE

One of the most important facilities in a training yard is an all-weather surface for schooling. Some people are lucky enough to be able to use their fields all year round, but unfortunately we live in an area which is predominantly clay, and this limits fieldwork to the dry summer months. Since we have had an outdoor school built it has made life much easier, and saves so much time; before, we used to hack to a school at the end of the road and also made use of the local indoor schools on a regular basis, but all this was very time-consuming. A fellow professional told us that later on, we would wonder how we had managed before, and advised us to make the school as big as possible right away, rather than making it merely adequate, though with the option to extend later on – it is surprising how little room there is when riding a big horse in a standard-sized school. One side of our school follows the curve-shaped line of the field which is ideal for teaching an animal to go deep on an inside bend. The school itself is predominantly square-shaped rather than oblong with two narrow sides. This allows us to ride and lunge a few at the same time, and when doing circle work it gives more scope. Although fenced with solid fencing on two sides it is not totally enclosed like some schools; animals are therefore more likely to keep interested and can see things around them while working.

Many people work to a price when having a school built, but in doing so, risk skimping on the basic principles such as proper drainage. There is nothing worse than spending thousands of pounds on a school, then having to have it re-dug and drained again after twelve months because the job was rushed in the first place. In many ways the foundations are more important than the type of surface you require, and drainage is definitely the most important consideration; as our school is situated next to a stream our drainage pipes go into this.

As for surfaces, there are so many to choose from – look in any horsey magazine and you are spoilt for choice! The best policy is to ask manufacturers if you can go and look at some of the work they have done in the locality, and ask the customers themselves if they are happy and if any problems have cropped up. We use wood chips, but many friends are using sand very happily. We kept the cost of our school down by using local people who were able to guarantee all the work, unlike many major firms who will generally only stand by the actual surface as most of the construction work is sub-contracted.

Constructing a manège is basically quite simple and some people have even built their own; one person bought a JCB very cheaply, dug out all the foundations with it and even used it to lift railway sleepers to the edges; he then sold it for a profit which paid for the school itself! Providing the surface is maintained and raked on a regular basis, especially if you are doing a lot of jumping on it, an all-weather surface is a very valuable asset and will last a long time.

STABLES AND STABLE MANAGEMENT

Stable Design

When building a stable block or converting farm buildings, remember to have a wide range of sizes to accommodate all shapes and heights. A lot of people who have been in ponies have to start all over again when they go up into horses. If you need boxes for foaling they must be as big as possible. We have two corner boxes 18×12ft (5.5×3.5m) which we use for this and for any big horses, although most of the time we make them into two 12.2hh boxes by installing a temporary partition. All stables must have adequate ventilation without being draughty; the traditional stable windows are still very much favoured since they allow fresh air in without draughts, essential if you are shutting top doors and putting up heat lamps for Wembley. Make sure the windows in your stables have bars for protection, and preferably non-splintering glass – I have seen a horse put his legs through a window when rolling. If using bars, make sure they are close enough together so feet do not get trapped between them.

All our feed mangers are white plastic corner ones, which are easy to keep clean and can be taken out of the frame should it be necessary for animals to be fed in them from the floor.

Good lighting is essential in a well-run stable yard both inside the stables – especially when you are busy plaiting a pony in the early hours of the morning – and outside, particularly in the horsebox area when loading and unloading when it is dark. I do not like to see electrical points inside a stable, so ours are situated outside the actual stable and sheltered from the rain by the overhang.

Hay

Hay racks are very convenient providing you have them at the right height for the particular animal; however, if they are too high for ponies then you will help develop unwanted muscle underneath the neck, and if too low for horses, the sections of hay can be taken out from the top. There is nothing worse than seeing hay scattered all over the bedding – quite apart from the fact that it is too expensive these days to waste. Muscle can also be made to develop the wrong way if small ponies have to reach over a door to be able to see out – however, do not have the doors so low that they can jump over!

We also use haynets and make sure that they are kept as high as possible – my pony, Snailwell Charles, loved jumping into them if they slipped down at all. We have two rings in each box, one for the haynet and the other by the manger – this is very useful when feeding a pony which has been plaited. We never leave them untied once plaited, as this breaks the hair and leaves the plaits sprutty. We also tie string in a loop to the metal rings thus making a second, string ring, so that if youngsters do pull back they will – hopefully! – break the string and not bring down the stable wall!

Water

We use big plastic buckets for water, which usually remain at least half full all day – the normal size ones are not large enough, especially for horses which on return from exercise, drink a lot. They are topped up at midday and refilled with fresh water at 'doing-up time' at about 3.30pm. A clean bucket is used to obtain water from a tank in the yard, and then used to pour the water into the stable buckets, rather than the stable buckets going straight into the tank; this keeps the water cleaner. If you have the type of animal who kicks buckets over – we usually have a couple of these hooligans each season – we lift the buckets off the floor using a clip and rope; we have found that these offending ponies can dislodge even the heaviest of buckets, like oak ones. Sometimes we remove the bucket handle and slot the bucket inside the corner manger – one particular pony used to swing his bucket until it was empty when it was held by a rope. The golden rule is to make sure water is fresh and the buckets are kept clean and not allowed to become slimy.

Beds and Bedding

We have the beds banked quite high at the sides to help prevent animals from getting cast. Make sure that there is plenty of bedding so that the concrete floor is not exposed; this can result in horses getting capped hocks when getting up and down. In fact for half the year our straw boxes are only mucked out properly once a week; by properly I mean the corners, sides and around the manger, and the latter is especially important – if horses discover old food which has been tossed out of the manger maybe days before and eat it, it could cause colic. These areas are all too frequently missed. On the other days these boxes are skipped out and freshly bedded twice daily – in other words semi-deep litter. This method gives the bed some substance for those animals which are prone to getting knocks, and provides extra warmth during the winter months.

For those animals on a diet or with respiratory problems, we use good quality shavings as an alternative to wheat straw; again, these boxes are religiously skipped out twice a day and 'bottomed' once a week. We have also used peat and paper as substitute bedding materials and found that peat became wet very easily but could be used in the garden afterwards, whereas paper worked very well with the cleaner ponies but was a nuisance to get rid of afterwards.

Stable Vices

Horses are like people, and their boredom threshold varies; in an ideal yard there should be enough going on to stop an animal from getting bored, either by watching the various activities, or in his own daily routine. However, we have had to put up tyres and on some occasions beach balls in the stable for some of them to play with, particularly the youngsters and especially colts.

In an enclosed yard like ours, if any vices do occur we have to try and eliminate or curb them to some extent. We have permanent weaving grills on two of the stable doors which have been more than adequate; alternatives to grills include dangling two bricks in sacking in the doorway, or putting a post in the middle of the doorway to decrease the area of swing. If the animal is a really bad weaver, and can weave even in the middle of the stable, you have no choice but to tie it up most of the time, as with a very bad box-walker; which is similar to being in a stall. Crib-biting and windsucking can be eliminated to some extent by putting cribbox or creosote on all the surfaces which they can grab. One well-known stud used to have a stable completely tiled so there were no protruding surfaces at all; but then again, not all animals require a surface – some of the older ponies do it as a habit. Providing it does not give them colic, it may be better to let them get on with it, though preferably in a stable situated in a secluded area of the yard so that younger animals do not have the opportunity to copy. Other people use muzzles with windsuckers, and special straps which resemble instruments of mediaeval torture to help 'cure' this problem.

The Daily Routine

Horses are creatures of habit and soon become accustomed to a set routine. Although it is difficult to keep to a set time on show days, since you will be getting up earlier and arriving back well after dark, it is essential that the yard itself runs to a normal daily timetable. Some highly strung horses have been known to get colic because they have been fed at different times.

As we have no live-in staff we start the yard a little later than most in the morning, at 8am. The horses are fed and hayed and mucked out which usually finishes between 9.00 and 9.30am; after a half-hour coffee break, they are exercised and turned out (all before lunch-time if possible), and some are also groomed and strapped. Lunchtime lasts an hour and varies from 12.00 to 2.00pm. In the afternoon, all the jobs are finished (which can include some tack cleaning) by 'doing-up time' at about 3.30pm. This consists of skipping out the beds, giving fresh water and hay, checking rugs and then feeding – this is normally only the second feed of the day since feeds are given at lunchtime only to those that have missed breakfast by being turned out. At the end of the working day the yard is left 'spick and span', looking as though nobody has been in at all since the evening before.

Tidiness

Keeping a stable-yard tidy is important because it reflects the standard of workmanship, and this is important if clients are visiting. Some yards even spend a half-day a week spring cleaning. It is extremely hard work keeping on top of the mowing, sweeping out feedrooms and tackrooms, washing out mangers, washing doors and windows, weeding the gravel, raking driveways etc, especially during the busy show season; but nothing gives more satisfaction when returning from a show than arriving at a very tidy stable-yard.

Staff

The ideal yard with every facility is all very fine, but without the good people to make it function well all is lost. Even if you are working with a yard full of champions (and given time it is surprising how much knowledge can be gained even by just grooming good animals) the work is routine and mundane so top class grooms need to be dedicated and to really enjoy working with horses. A lot of young people only see the showing part when applying for a job in a show yard, and are not aware of the hard work which is involved. When interviewing recruits, I always make a point of telling them how hard the work can be, almost to the point of putting them off.

As with all jobs, some survive, others last only a couple of days. Personal recommendation is usually a foolproof way of obtaining good staff. We have had some very good people, including some YTS students, who have handled the animals well and kept their sense of humour whilst working extremely hard. One hears stories of grooms who haven't had a day off for months on end, which is ridiculous – everybody needs a break each week; we are great believers in this, and maintain that the grooms return to the yard refreshed and relaxed. One of the biggest problems is that some of the new grooms do not realise that although you want a job done well, you also want it done quickly. I have seen one girl take all morning to muck out one box and then take all afternoon to groom one small pony – needless to say, she didn't last long!

The success of any yard relies heavily on teamwork; if at times we have been busy, our older jockeys have given us tremendous help and in return have learnt a lot themselves. Jockeys who just arrive a bare ten minutes before a class learn very little. If you have a busy showing week, it is most important to have reliable people in the yard getting the next string ready. We usually have one girl working with our head girl and a good YTS student as well, apart from a posse of part-time help, especially at weekends. All are instructed to be firm with the animals in a quiet manner – one of the problems often encountered is that of a nervous groom, since he or she can easily frighten the animal, especially if they shout at every situation. We have such a wide selection of animals in our yard, ranging from lead-rein ponies to big hunters, including Arab stallions, that all our girls must be capable of looking after every size and type.

FEEDING

Even though feeding is becoming more and more scientific, it is still very much an art, and something defined by personal skill. I have no intention of dictating specific feeding regimes as each animal is an individual with its own special requirements. I tend to keep my feeding very basic and simple for two reasons: first, you can always add to it, and secondly, when away at shows you have to pass on that feed list to other people.

Concentrates

I usually feed sugar beet, bran, chop and whatever else is required in the morning, and a hot feed at night, either with water from the tank in the feedroom or with the linseed and barley cooked on the stove (also in the feedroom). How many mothers do you hear complaining that the linseed boiled over again on the hob in the kitchen – and you can't blame them, it's such messy stuff. The sugar beet must be soaked overnight in warm water and in winter with hot water so that it is not ice cold in the morning, which could give rise to colic – perhaps keep the bucket in the kitchen overnight.

For fattening food, I like to use Bailey's non-heating feedstuffs and the micronised, cooked, flaked barley. When using oats, try to remember that the art of feeding is to give according to the work done and the job the pony or horse is intended for – a lead-rein pony won't want the same quantity of corn that a heavy working horse will require.

When showing horses, there is nothing better for the judge than to sit on a well-schooled, fit horse; however, as ponies are often ridden by less competent jockeys and are sometimes quite highly strung anyway, they are not required to be as fit. Often ponies are just fed bulk to keep them the right shape; as the season progresses they get themselves fit anyway – again, it depends on the individual pony. There are those ponies who seem to get fat on fresh air, and if these must be on a diet they can always have a feed topped up with carrots to make it a little more interesting. Carrots are the most nutritional diuretic and so are ideal for horses that are on a lot of corn. Fed whole they are also ideal for the animal which bolts its food.

Boiled food, especially a porridge mix with oats, is best for putting weight on, although you must always bear in mind not to feed some ponies too much protein as you could have problems with laminitis. Similarly, never feed an animal the same amount of concentrates if it is doing less work than usual, as this can lead to azoturia. We have also experimented with soya meal, under the guidance of a nutritionist. Bran mashes are given once a week, usually the night before a day off; otherwise the animals are fed twice daily with an extra feed at night if required – the golden rule is to feed little and often. One of the most common mistakes, which we have all made, is that when moving from ponies to horses we haven't given the latter enough feed, still thinking in terms of ponies instead of horses; just as some horsemen have their ponies too fat.

Hay

Getting good hay can be a problem, and for horses with a respiratory problem (very common nowadays) most people are using Horsehage; it is much higher in protein than hay, and you need feed only a quarter the amount – special haynets are now available with smaller holes to make it last longer. Being a feeder who judges the shape by eye, I am always changing the hay list – and you have probably gathered by now that we have a multitude of lists around the yard; this does mean, however, that everyone working in the yard can do all the jobs competently.

Supplements

Feeding vitamins is a pet subject of mine, for two reasons: I am involved with an extremely good range of products; and secondly, we had a positive dope test with one of our 14.2hh ponies in 1980 after winning the Great Yorkshire Show Championship. Caffeine, which is a stimulant, was detected; this arose from the cocoa husk in the mineral supplement we had been using for a number of years. The moral of the story is that people must be aware of what they are feeding to their animals, especially those which may be subjected to a random dope test at the major shows. Although the expense of carrying out these controversial tests is very high, most societies, and especially the BSPS, see it as a necessary step towards policing the sport.

Food quality today is so poor that vitamin supplements play a necessary part in feeding, and in our experience we have found certain nutrients ideal for certain circumstances. Garlic and seaweed are very good for laminitis cases; garlic and honey for animals with respiratory problems, and vitamin E has been fed successfully with alkaline syrup for animals prone to azoturia. We prefer to use the liquid vitamin supplements as opposed to the powder form, as they seem to have better results. However, vitamins can only be used as a supplement and not as a substitute for good feeding. Horses look well outside only if they are well inside. Regular worming is essential; we do it every eight weeks, and change the wormer from one make to another to avoid resistance building up.

GROOMING

No matter how well you groom your exhibits, if the animals are not blooming from inside they will not shine outside. Between shows our animals spend a lot of time outside in the field, and it is almost impossible to get them totally clean by just brushing alone so before a show they often get a bath. It is imperative that you do keep on top of the grooming as best as you can in case, for instance, it is too cold to bath. Good grooming and strapping also give a depth of shine which cannot be substituted with regular bathing when the natural oils are washed away. One way of doing both on a cold day is to wet the animal with a piece of sacking dampened in hot water, called an Irish sponge, and then dry it by body brushing.

When grooming, so many people forget to brush the legs and the heads properly and more importantly the nooks and crannies like between the legs, the girth region and behind the ears. Any dried sweat or mud ignored can lead to irritation and result in girth galls and other problems, especially with the more quality stock which has sensitive skin.

We seldom brush the tail out as this may cause thinning and when we do, we use only a soft brush like a hair brush or body brush.

Procedure

Of all the body brushes, I find the best ones are those with leather backing (as opposed to the wood ones) as there is less chance of banging knees and hocks with these. The procedure we adopt is to use a rubber curry comb, then dandy brush for any mud and dirt, and then body brush, remembering to brush under the belly and the two-way hair system at the end of the rib cage. We then sponge the face and dock and water-brush the mane and tail (putting on a bandage) and the rest of the body. Whilst this is drying we pick out the feet, remembering to clean the frog and heel region as well. The best hoof-picks are those with a small brush on the back. Hoof oil is applied inside and out, and at the same time the foot is checked for any risen clenches or loose shoes. The animal is then strapped dry with either a leather strapper or a hay wisp or stable rubber before a final wipe down with a cloth.

Strapping

When strapping, the regions to concentrate on are the top of the neck (but not at the poll or just above the wither), the top of the quarters, the flank region and the buttock area – but definitely *not* the shoulder or loin regions. Some nervous animals and young-sters do not take kindly to strapping at first so be careful not to make them afraid or to get kicked yourself. Strapping should be done firmly and rhythmically – the timing should be so that you can see the muscle twitch about every second. It is commonsense not to strap the crest of the neck if it is already overtopped – you want to create a rainbow shape. Similarly if the quarters are sunken at the sides or there are poverty marks along the buttocks, concentrate more on these areas. In the production of a show animal it is important to strap correctly; you can, for instance, improve the look of a low set-on tail carriage with a well muscled quarter. But as with exercise, muscle development will be nil if the animal is not well covered with flesh in the first place.

Electric Groomers

If you are going to purchase an electric groomer the one with the revolving brush-head is the best; some stables have them on a runner system suspended from the ceiling which keeps the wires and machine from off the floor. These machines tone the muscles as well, but be careful not to catch manes and tails in the revolving brush – not the best way to pull them!

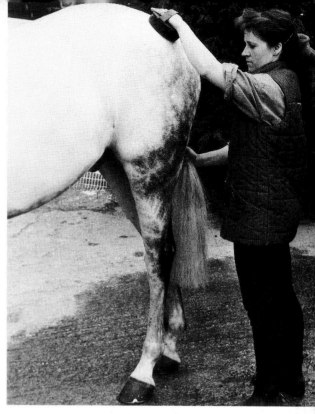

Strapping: (Left) The top of the neck
(Above) The top of the quarters
(Below) The flank region

CLOTHING

A cotton sheet next to the coat will keep it cool and dust-free; although bed sheets are useful, these need to be well folded back and secured otherwise they only last a short while and will finish on the floor badly torn. If they slip back around the roller region they can rub the hair and make this area very sore. If possible use an old summer sheet, one that is too tatty for the shows, and in summer this is often all a pony will need whilst it is stabled during hotter days.

The ideal blankets are the big Witney ones that cover the animal well. Although people do say that layers of clothing are better for maintaining warmth, I believe the practical answer is to use one good quality blanket than lots of silly thin ones which take a good half-hour to put on and which slip when the animal moves. If you are putting on a lot more layers either at the beginning of the season to sweat the coat out, or at the end of the season to keep the summer coat in, it may be better to use continental quilts (from the market) or old sleeping bags, as this will reduce the weight factor of the clothing.

If forming a collar with the blanket either under the top rug or over, be careful that there is not too much pressure on the mane which may then rub and fall out. Some people use a piece of sheepskin pad around the wither region to prevent this happening, just as you would if the rug rubs the hair around the chest region.

There are so many types of night rug on the market these days that one is spoilt for choice. Those requiring a separate roller are useful as the roller can then also be used with just a cotton sheet when the animal is warm. The thick quilted rugs are lovely and warm and there is often no need for woollen blankets as well, but they are often too hot in summer. The Lavenham type rugs are better if they have a cool cotton-type lining rather than nylon as there is less chance of the animal breaking into a sweat with cotton. Of all the different sorts of special fastening, we have found that the best are the partially elasticated straps which allow you an extra pull before fastening, and the rugs which have the surcingles attached at the wither (where the front of the saddle would be) and over the quarters (just behind where the back of the saddle would be). The problem with the cross-over straps is that sometimes the back ones may pull the back of the rug more forwards, but the advantage of these surcingles is that they do take the pressure off the back. Whether you use these or the old-

A continental quilt and rug: a useful alternative to blankets

fashioned roller, we always put foam pads on the back under the roller, or under the girth-line where the roller touches the skin, or where the cross surcingles or parallel straps meet.

BACKS

This routine is followed on the advice of our back man who visits us twice a year; at the beginning of the season and again just before the BSPS Championships or Horse of the Year Show. Just as humans feel the odd twinge, so horses can just 'put something out' either in their school work or if they are merely galloping about in the field and stop abruptly. We had one animal which would not put on muscle in the right place until it had had a check-up and the problem was sorted out; another would not go on the correct bend, and consequently would not lead on the right leg in canter because there was some pressure on that side. Once or twice a ride on one of the hacks in the yard has felt uneven, and this has been corrected by the back man. He is an important member of a showing yard and a lot of the top professionals call upon his services.

TEETH

We also use a horse dentist who again visits the yard about twice a year. We produce so many new animals, if one isn't eating very well or has a mouth problem in its schooling this could be due to a sharp edge or a wolf tooth, and it is reassuring to be able to eliminate the obvious. In schooling work, if a mouth problem persists and your dentist has given everything the all-clear then you know the problem is either mental or a habit and can be dealt with accordingly.

THE FOOT AND SHOEING

Perhaps one of the most important members of your showing team is the farrier, and a good, reliable one is a rarity indeed. We are fortunate to have an excellent chap who lives nearby, which is very convenient if a shoe is pulled off at the last minute, say the day before an important show. A good farrier can improve a show animal's action beyond recognition, and if ever an animal is lame and the trouble can be easily diagnosed as in the foot, we always call the farrier rather than the vet. We prefer the wide showing aluminium plates in front with light steels behind, rather than the very narrow ones which soon wear thin at the toe; for big horses, and those having a lot of road work, light steels are far more sensible. Too few exhibitors in my opinion appreciate the importance of well shod feet when showing, and they wait until the shoes are dropping off before they call the blacksmith.

VETERINARY HELP

No exhibitor of top class animals can operate efficiently without a good horse vet, one who is up to date with the latest drugs and who will be able to tell you more about the risks of dope-testing when an animal is still under his supervision. During the season you want an animal off the circuit for as short a time as possible. Without going into detail about certain ailments, each yard must have a well stocked veterinary cupboard both in the yard and in the horsebox, so that certain minor accidents can be handled either without the vet or until he arrives – for example, wound dressing powder, gamgee, stretchy elasticated bandage, poultices, colic drench; some of the better veterinary kits available at a good saddler's contain ice pack bandages and are well worth the money.

CERTIFICATES AND REGISTRATIONS

After the New Year, there is a lot of office work involved; for instance, making sure vaccination certificates are available for renewal – our boosters are given usually around Christmas time since there is less activity over the festive period. Check with your vet that the certificates are valid for shows like the RIHS and Wembley; you will not be able to compete if they do not meet the requirements, even if they are only out of date by one day. Also check that there is an identification chart with the 'flu card.

Some show animals need to be measured at the beginning of the season for their height certificates, and it is amazing how many people do not prepare for this properly – which is stupid, as what use is a 14.2hh pony that measures ¼in over, or a small hunter that measures 15.2½in? Practice is important, because if a horse or pony is excited or agitated it will be literally 'on its toes' and will measure higher than when it is relaxed and 'flat'. By practising at home, this will accustom a young or nervous animal to a stranger using a measuring stick and will also give some idea as to how much may need to be taken off his feet. One of the most difficult types to measure is the highly strung animal which is up to height, especially with the present system which entails travelling to the vet's premises. Unless you have your animal relaxed by working him hard before the journey, you stand little chance of having him 'flat' on arriving at strange premises. To be fair to the vet, he is not there to catch you out, and most will give an animal sufficient time to relax before recording the measurement; but it is up to the owner to make sure that he has done his homework properly. However, if a vet suspects that there has been any malpractice, either by doping or putting the animal under any undue stress, he will refuse to measure.

The next step is to get your membership renewed and your exhibit registered with the appropriate societies so that you can quote the numbers on your entry forms. It is important to put all the correct details on the forms and only fair to the breeder to give him recognition if appropriate. Once the schedules have arrived in the post, keeping up with the office work is a full time job. We have a large desk diary in which the days of the shows are recorded with the names of the judges and most importantly the closing date of entries. At the beginning of each week I can therefore see what entries are due, and once the entries are recorded, can also work out from its pages which animals are travelling where that particular month.

PLANNING THE SEASON

We usually split the season into two, shows leading up to the Royal International Horse Show and shows leading up to the Horse of the Year Show; most owners want to qualify for these two major shows so our system is geared to this. It is important that every animal is given every chance to qualify which means that for the first six or seven shows everything is entered more or less on spec, which is a costly business. However, it is better to be entered than to rely on only one or two selected shows just in case the animal in question goes lame or develops a cough at the time when it was planned to be shown. If you have one or two animals in the same class, and one has qualified already, there is not the same urgency these days under the present qualification system (the ticket being passed down the line) to keep this one at home, in the belief that it is stopping the other one. One of the cardinal sins in a showing yard is to miss entries at a show where an animal stood a very good chance. Some yards ask clients to do their own entries; however, we believe that it is better for the administration to do this so that all the organisation is under one roof, so to speak, and all the tickets arrive at the same place at the right time.

We are so fortunate in this sport to be able to compete at many different levels so that if things are not going according to plan, perhaps a show horse is just not developing as one would have hoped, you can go to a decent smaller show until he's ready for the big circuit. Similarly if a horse is misbehaving and you want to try something different, it is far better to experiment at a quieter show than in front of everybody, including a lot of judges, at the Royal or suchlike. The tip is to cut your suit according to your cloth; it is the trainer's responsibility in a showing ring to have an exhibit prepared and placed at the right show so that it stands the best possible chance of being successful.

CHAPTER 4

Schooling

Proper schooling will enable the handler to have a greater degree of control, and the training procedure should be seen simply as a matter of communication between the horse and rider. From early on, the horse must learn to have respect for the handler, he must learn to be tied up, led from A to B, learn to stand quietly when being groomed, and to stand to one side when his feed is being brought into the stable. When horses are spoilt and allowed to get away with murder, particularly in the stable, this is where problems begin.

BREAKING IN

The time for breaking depends on the owner: some people do it at two years old or in the spring of the three-year-old year so that the animal can be shown under saddle after 1 July. In general, the normal time is at the back end of the three-year-old year. Unfortunately, many animals are broken in when they are neither mentally or physically ready to undertake such a task, and 'breaking' in these cases has a more literal meaning. However, it seems stupid to rush this early part of an animal's education – this is the basis for all further training: how many times does one hear of an animal having to be re-broken? In the past, ponies were broken at an older age and up to twelve months' work was put into the breaking and making of an animal. This could be the reason why so many good ponies do not seem to last the course these days, as compared to the Valentino ponies which took a while to mature but stayed in the show ring for a very long time. As Count Orssich said 'Production is far too hurried'; the reason perhaps being that we live in a very commercial world and owners are preoccupied with costs and values; besides which in junior classes, jockeys have only a limited amount of time in the respective classes – particularly as children do seem to be getting bigger these days.

When you decide to break an animal, make sure that you are able to spend an hour a day for at least six to eight weeks on the job, as continuity at this stage is vital. If you cannot afford this sort of time, or feel that the job is beyond your own capabilities, then consider sending the animal away to a professional yard; one which is not too busy will be the best.

One of the most important things to do is to make a mouth – an animal with a good mouth will always have a job as a ridden animal, even if not in the show ring; but a horse with no mouth will never be an enjoyable ride. The normal breaking bit is one with keys in the middle so that the animal is encouraged to play with them and salivate correctly. I like to replace this bit with a padded snaffle bit as soon as possible because I feel that after a certain length of time, the keys encourage an animal to get its tongue over the bit. Similarly the old-fashioned wooden bit with holes in, which encourage the horse to suck on it, can sometimes lead the animal to windsuck.

When putting on a bridle for the very first time (even for showing in-hand), prior to breaking proper, it is better to put the actual bridle on first and then put the bit in the mouth, and fasten it to the end of the cheek pieces; this way you will not have the animal fidgeting whilst you put the bridle on over his ears because you have the bit too high in his mouth. Make sure the bit fits well, and that it is not too low in his mouth as this will also encourage him to roll his tongue over the bit. If your animal is prone to this, even when older, having a noseband on fairly tight will stop him from opening his mouth. Let your youngster become accustomed to the bridle in his stable for a few days, making sure that he cannot catch either bridle or bit on any protruding objects.

The next stage is to introduce him to a roller, which must be well padded and tightened up very gradually, although if your youngster has been rugged up for showing he will already know about this article; it is the putting on and removing of the roller which most frightens the horse. Once he is quite accustomed to it, you can put side-reins on, from the bit to the roller, not too tight or too slack, but enough for him to have a contact – and of course they must both be the same length. If the roller has a tendency to slip back use a breast plate, and if it moves forward use a crupper (making sure that you put a tail bandage on first to prevent rubbing) – again like the roller, not too tight or the pony will have a bucking fit! Some old horsemen advocate using pillar reins attached to a horse in tack in a stall, and say that this is the best way to make a mouth.

LUNGEING

Depending on the animal, it may be wiser to teach him to lunge with just a cavesson to begin with, unless he is extremely difficult or works in a bad shape and then he would work better with tack on. In normal circumstances, introduce the tack at a later stage when he is relaxed and working well on the lunge. Lungeing is a vital part of a horse's education; in some yards it is merely a way of teaching the horse to understand voice commands (particularly important with smaller ponies) and a necessary part of the process of breaking, whereas in other yards it is the most important activity in the overall production, because it is like riding from the ground, and enables the handler to observe how much the horse thinks for himself, which is especially useful when jumping. I myself have been taught to school from on top, but I realise how important a part lungeing can play in production, particularly with youngsters, as it teaches the horse to balance itself and develop a sense of rhythm without the weight of a rider; it is also good for improving action and muscle development. However, many youngsters are lunged too much on hard ground, in my opinion, and this results in worn joints and lameness through strenuous exercise. Lungeing can also be useful to take the edge off a sharp animal prior to going into the ring.

All our animals are lunged at least once a week. The cavesson should be lightweight and supple, strong and above all well fitting – so many of them shift during lungeing and rub the eyes because the throat-lash hasn't been secure enough. If used in conjunction with a bridle, put the cavesson over the bridle but with the noseband fastening under the cheek pieces to avoid interference with the bit. Lunge lines should be long enough and should be attached to the middle ring to encourage forward movement – as with side-reins, make sure that the clips are not too heavy as they can put undue pressure on the mouth and nose region.

At the human end, if circling left, the rein should be held in the left hand with the excess loops and the whip in the other, with the thumbs on top and certainly never wrapping the line around the hand or allowing it to drag on the floor. Reverse this position when circling right. When describing a circle, try not to hold the line with too much tension; it should not be like an iron rod. The lunge whip with a thong is an aid, not an instrument of punishment; it should be treated with respect by both parties, and if it is to work to its full advantage, make sure it is long enough. We always use brushing boots all round, rather than bandages

which can slip or tighten when wet, with the buckles or velcro fasteners on the outside and the buckles fastening towards the tail end. These will not only protect but will give extra support, particularly with youngsters or if working very hard with older animals.

As with ridden work, it is better to achieve fifteen minutes good work than to spend an hour getting nowhere. The annoying animals are those which take ten minutes to settle, work well for two minutes then become extremely tired. When lungeing, keep yourself and the whip within the angle formed by the lunge line controlling the head, and the whip controlling the hindquarters, and look towards the point of the shoulder. The first time lungeing is done (you may require an assistant), do it in an enclosed area to lessen the risk of the horse wandering or escaping. Stand in the middle and allow your assistant to lead him round in a small circle at walk (from the near side on the left rein and vice versa on the right rein). The person in the middle should give the commands which should be firm and comprehensive – at no time should a conversation be held with a third person. Once the horse has got used to the idea, ask him to trot on, using

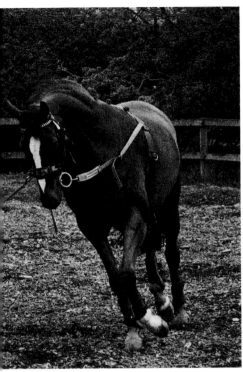

It is important to keep within the angle when lungeing so that you can control the head and hindquarters

a flick of the whip and your voice – be careful that your assistant doesn't get left behind which will increase his chances of getting cow-kicked.

When the animal is confident and understands the basic principles and can determine between walk and trot, the assistant can gradually leave his side and come nearer to the middle on the left rein, encouraging the animal to become more independent. At first lunge in larger circles, keeping him between your two hands and encouraging free forward movement and a nice steady rhythm. Perfect the walk and trot before you attempt canter. Many animals find this pace difficult at this stage – you will find this out from the way he copes when on the odd occasion he breaks to canter when in trot.

Just as humans write with one hand, so horses are also one-sided, bending better on one rein than the other; the 'hard' side will eventually need more work to make it more supple. Once the pony has learnt to balance himself – which you can tell more from watching the inside hind leg, rather than the front ones – you can gradually collect his work by making the circles smaller.

The next stage is for him to work in his tack, but allow him to work loose in his side-reins before gradually tightening them up. The object of side-reins is to encourage a correct head carriage thereby achieving a good outline; it is not to tie them in, which will force an artificial head carriage or make him bend unnaturally, both of which will cause him to stiffen and evade, quite apart from ruining his mouth. With a good breaking roller you can attach the side-reins higher or lower to counteract too low or too high a head carriage.

Some horses take to lungeing like ducks to water and lunge well all their lives; you can lunge these collectedly in a small circle and then use all the schooling area to open them out on a longer rein. However, if you are having problems, it is far safer to keep the circle smaller and work within an enclosed area. Try not to have your line too long, then if an animal does try to shoot off, you have less chance of being dragged; go with him some of the way so that he has nothing to pull against. If he becomes very strong, make a simple gag by attaching the end of the line to the outside ring of the bit, then bring it through the head-piece and down through the other bit-ring to your hand. If the horse suddenly stops and faces in, it is because he is going behind the movement (one common cause of this is over-tight side-reins) and you must use your lunge whip more effectively to drive the hindquarters up so that he accepts the bit more. Another problem may be that he will not halt straightaway: keep your patience and make your voice commands more determined, and at the same time give a simple tug on the lunge line (just as you would flick the whip to encourage more impulsion). If this does not work, make him run into a non-jumpable hedge or wall, at the same time saying 'halt'.

It is important that at any time a horse learns to stand for a while when on the lunge. If the horse falls in on the lunge (it could be that your circle is too small) use your whip to push the shoulder out; similarly if he leans out, use your whip to push the quarters out. At all times the person lungeing must anticipate the horse's next move and be quick in his reactions; just as the person who advocates long-reining must be quick on his feet and with his hands if he is to follow through with the horse and not get the reins in a tangle.

Champion Hack Duke of Newcastle, Small Hack of the Year, 1985 – particularly remembered by the author, who once showed him, for his exceptional ride and good limbs

Long-reining

The art of long-reining is a lot more difficult to achieve than lungeing and some people never master it, even though they may be quite accomplished at lungeing. The trainer must have light, sensitive hands (though as someone once said, it is no use having good hands if there isn't a brain to go with them) since the contact is directly on the horse's mouth and its effect is exaggerated because of the longer reins. Many people consider that this is the important stage between lungeing and backing as it teaches the horse to go more forward from behind. However, far more harm than good can be done if long-reining is not executed well.

BACKING

When you think the horse is ready to be backed, change the roller for the saddle, but without stirrups – the side-reins can be attached either to the girth straps or the D-rings. Lunge the horse for a couple of days to let him get used to the noise of the saddle flaps. After that, put some leathers and irons on the saddle, fastened up to begin with, but allowing them to unravel as the horse works. Eventually the animal will grow accustomed to long stirrups clanking at his side. At Blue Slate we then get rid of the side-reins and replace them with proper reins which fasten through the stirrup irons; in addition to this we attach a running martingale, as the neck-strap is very useful when the time comes to get on board the horse. Now the animal is ready for backing.

It is important that the trainer takes charge at the head, since the horse is most accustomed to his voice, with a rider and his assistant by the saddle. In an enclosed space to begin with, give the rider a leg-up so that he just lies across the saddle whilst the trainer pats and talks to the horse. Depending on the reaction, do this a few times, then walk the horse around with the rider lying on the saddle and the assistant holding his leg.

All being well, and providing the horse isn't startled at all by the shifting weight of the rider and remains quite relaxed, he is ready to be ridden astride. A this point we usually lead him – with

Rye Tangle (Hack of the Year, 1985–7). His outstanding quality and presence is evident as he heads the line up at the Royal Windsor Show above Westhill Carmen and Jim Bean

The lead rein classes are a delight to watch; the trick is to create the right picture for the judges

Long-reining teaches the horse to go forward from behind

the rider on board – around the yard and then into the school, where he is eventually led at trot like a lead-rein pony. Soon afterwards the person leading can lengthen the lunge line and adopt a lungeing situation at walk and then trot. Once the team is happy, the lunge line is detached and the horse is ridden solo, in circles at first with the trainer in the centre so that the horse still thinks he is being lunged. The object of the exercise is to have the horse going forwards in a nice and steady, balanced working rhythm – although it may at first be less fluent than when without the rider. Once the horse is working around the outside track of the school by itself, accepting more contact and obedient to the leg, there is no looking back.

It is most important, in this backing stage, to strike the right balance, whereby you are making sufficient progress each day but are not frightening the horse by rushing, thereby endangering the safety of the rider involved.

Even when the horse has reached the riding-away stage, it may still be necessary to keep lungeing him; this can be reduced when

68

the team is more confident of his behaviour. One of the worst sights is that often seen at shows, of a pony being lunged at record-breaking speed in the hope of tiring it out – instead of which it is becoming increasingly tuned-up! Similarly it seems to be the fashion these days to long-rein lead-rein ponies on the showground, with mother, father and children all following on behind and looking like the 'Conga' at a party!

THE YOUNG HORSE: RIDING HIM AWAY

It is a great mistake to start schooling for the show ring too soon after breaking; an animal should either be turned away or allowed to see life a little more first. Problems will develop if schooling is rushed and before horses are both mentally and physically ready. If you are lucky enough to enjoy good hacking facilities, the youngster accompanied by a quieter, older horse will benefit more from this than anything else, opening gates, cantering along grass verges and even popping over a small hedge. This will fitten him up and broaden his education, teaching him to behave in a forward-thinking way. And it is surprising how much schooling can be done on the roads – some ponies switch off as soon as you go into the school and attempt any semblance of a circle, but respond to roadwork schooling. It is important to put on knee-boots for roadwork, in case of an accident, as broken knees are frowned on in the show ring.

If a horse is broken in the summer, it will do no harm to take him to a small quiet show to ride round, even if he has already seen the sights and sounds as an in-hand animal – the experience of having bandages on, and standing in a horsebox while others are loading and unloading, is all part of his education. You never know what will happen with even the quietest of animals until you get to a show, nor is there any way that you can recreate its atmosphere at home. We always take a novice animal to at least one show to look around before putting it in the ring, and then usually find a small, quiet affair to launch it. The people who put their animal straight in at, for example, Windsor or in an Open class, are very brave indeed – although some of the old school say that if an animal is good enough and ready, it shouldn't make any difference where it has its début.

Some people also advocate taking the young horse hunting; however, this can easily work in a negative way, particularly if the young animal becomes unsettled – and a bad experience at this stage could easily lead to problems later on.

PREPARING FOR A SHOW SEASON

Our ponies are usually broken in the autumn and ridden away so that they are ready to work with the more experienced animals after Christmas, when they will do slow hacking work to harden them up and get them fitter for work aimed at the show ring. The young animal being broken is better kept unfit until ready to do harder work; each one is an individual, however, and some will need to be fitter than others, which usually depends on physical ability and temperament, and the job it will have to do. For instance, a show hunter needs to be a lot fitter than a child's pony, as he has to gallop round the main ring several times on a show day, and an unfit horse can sometimes make a noise which could jeopardise your chances. Some horses, if shown in soft condition, will melt away after a few outings and look like toast-racks by mid-season; so it pays to have them hard fit to begin with and then let them down slightly, rather than never getting them fit in the first place. Remember that in most cases, horses will become fitter as the season progresses anyway, and if you get your horse too fit too soon, you can become caught in a Catch 22 situation – you have to work your horse in for hours before going into the ring, but this in turn is making him fitter again. In these cases it is better to turn the horse away for a few weeks and show him off grass, something which we would do with a very sharp show animal anyway.

Nothing looks better in a show ring than a well-produced horse which is obviously as fit as a fiddle; however, there is no point in coming to the show if it is going to give the judge too strong a ride or display excessively bad manners in a ridden pony class. On the other hand, horses are sometimes evasive simply because their owners have brought them to a show insufficiently fit for the physical demands of the work expected of them – in many ways this 'naughtiness' merely shows the need for a little more preparation.

We try to give our show animals as much variety as possible; once they are going well they spend most of the days between shows in the field, with a workout the day before a show. Many show horses and ponies suffer from too much schooling, and look bored with life and mechanical in their way of going. Our success with Gay Sovereign, who had become sick of showing, was because we simply took him out on hacks and even to the beach to renew his interest in life – it was certainly nothing to do with injections of caffeine which was whispered abroad following the positive dope test! The key to it all was simply to avoid schooling altogether, which works 90% of the time in such cases. It is also essential to do this if your animal is anticipating in his individual show. Then, of course, you have to find a way to school him without him knowing – usually on a hack. We had a pony who anticipated quite a lot, which lost him many a class in the process – this was because a previous owner had made him practise his show every night when the children came home from school!

Keeping a show animal fresh towards the end of the season is a difficult task, especially if it has travelled a lot during a hot summer. A particularly difficult period is the time between the August Bank Holiday shows and Wembley: some exhibitors have even taken a qualified animal cub-hunting so that it will be nice and fresh for Wembley!

PRACTICAL SCHOOLING FOR HORSE AND RIDER

Schooling is basically common sense, there is nothing magic about it – the magic is when the end result is perfection. People who take short cuts, a common problem these days, are only kidding themselves and will suffer the consequences later on. If a horse is good in his flat-work, he will be a pleasure to ride and will have the ability to achieve other things. When schooling for the show ring there are basically three main considerations: the horse must be balanced, he must be relaxed, and he must be going forwards between hand and leg in the hope of giving a judge and jockey a good ride (being relaxed is very important). Most show-ring work is based on the circle and involves transitions; this means that a lot of time must be spent on perfecting a correct bend, and the horse and rider must be capable of performing a sequence of smooth transitions well.

The rider must at all times be in complete control, with the horse going forwards in response to the rider's leg-aids, and engaging his hind legs which are the source of impulsion. The power thus created is contained by the rider each time he asks the horse to make a contact with the bit, the hands asking the horse to flex. The rider is said to have the horse 'between hand and leg' when the impulsion generated by his leg-aid has sufficient energy to be relayed through the hindquarters and the body to the head, and back along the reins to the rider's hands; this will create a good shape, with the horse's back rounded and the hind legs active, as long as the horse is relaxed and 'on the bit'. When he is 'above the bit', his head carriage is too high which results in a hollow back and lost impulsion. The horse is said to be 'behind the bit' when he is not going forward with sufficient energy, and is drawing his head in to his chest to avoid contact; a stronger leg-aid is therefore needed to push him up to the bridle. Head carriage always comes from behind and is a natural progression. In most novice horses the general carriage is lower and longer, but develops as the young horse learns to work more strongly from behind.

Straightness and Suppleness

In the forward paces, the horse must track up and the rider must aim for straightness; the horse must neither lean in, nor swing the quarters out and the rider must control this with the hand and leg. When turning, the horse should move along the line of the turn as a complete unit, without showing any signs of stiffness. A pony that moves in rhythm is a balanced pony – those with natural balance are a pleasure to train. If this is not the case, then it is up to the trainer to help establish a steady rhythm which is comfortable for the horse; neither too fast nor too slow – work over trotting poles is invaluable in achieving this. If a horse is too onward bound, it is better not to keep pulling him back as this will upset the momentum, but perform a half-halt: this 'freezes' the movement so to speak – as if executing a downward transition, close the hand and keep the horse steady (without pulling) for a couple of steps, holding the movement with the seat, back and legs to meet the contact; then allow him forwards again. A half-halt can be used whenever you need to call the horse to attention: before turns and transitions, and in all paces, so it is obviously very useful in the show ring, particularly when riding in crowded conditions (such as the tent at Wembley).

Lazy and young horses will learn to go more forwards in straight lines and in a larger area; horses which go too fast will slow down if you work in smaller circles, though remember that the tighter the circle, the more impulsion will be needed if an even rhythm is to be maintained – something which a lot of riders fail to do when showing in an indoor arena or small ring. Corners in a ring or arena should be treated as quarter circles, and even though at times you may need to ride deep into the corner you must maintain the bend and keep the movement flowing – do not head straight for the rope and then turn the pony's head sharply at right-angles. A circle is a line with continuous bend; there are no straight lines in a true one, and if you were to put a true circle in a square track it should only touch the track at points north, south, east and west.

When asking a pony to bend, he should bend from your inside leg and not just with his head, with the forelimbs and hindlimbs moving forward on the same track. If you just pull at his head to turn, his quarters will swing out off the track or he will lean in. Your outside leg behind the girth will correct the quarters, and your inside leg should keep the horse on the track and prevent him leaning in. When asking for bend, squeeze with the inside hand (you should be able to see the horse's inside eye) whilst the inside leg on the girth creates the impulsion and around which the horse is bending, with the outside leg resting against the horse ready in case the hindquarters swing out. The outside hand is there to regulate the pace if necessary. It is important that you keep your hands independent of each other and at either side of the horse's neck so that the messages through the bit remain clear. All horses are one-sided and will naturally take an incorrect, outside bend on the 'hard' side; as with lungeing, more work is therefore needed on the weaker rein, since one-sidedness is something which judges look for when horses are asked to change the rein in the ring, and of course when they ride an exhibit. Moreover, if the horse bends correctly there is a much better chance of striking off on the right leg at canter.

Transitions

Transitions must be smooth, like going up and down in a lift. Warn your pony with a half-halt a second or two before you actually want the change of pace, making sure that he is listening to your legs. There is nothing worse than seeing a child flapping its legs or pulling at the reins in mild panic because the transition has not been prepared in advance. If the horse is relaxed and on the bit, with his hocks well underneath and keeping a steady contact, his basic shape should not change through the transition; perhaps the most common sight is seeing a pony come off the bit, sometimes through soreness or because the rider is being too hard with his hands and is not giving at the required moment. When going from halt to walk and walk to trot, both legs should be applied; when asking for canter, it may be advisable to half-halt first – make sure you have the correct bend, then, with the inside leg on the girth and the outside one behind, urge the horse forwards with seat and legs. When making this transition the rider must not tip forwards or lean in as this could upset the horse's balance and result in him striking off on the wrong leg.

When coming down through transitions, half-halt and with the legs, back and seat, push the horse into a resistant hand; keep the animal balanced so that it does not 'run' through the transition. At the first sign of the next gear, push the horse forwards so that he doesn't fall in a heap. Often in an individual show one sees a sequence of downward transitions which are not smooth and tidy, and it looks as if the animal has ground to a halt. A rider will very often get left behind whilst executing transitions, especially when coming down from a faster pace.

The Walk

I do like to see a good walk: this is the pace which gives the judge the first and the final impression. It is also the most difficult pace to cultivate, and can easily be ruined, either because the rider allows the horse to go behind the movement which results in a 'shuffle', giving the impression of a short front and a choppy stride; or he can make the animal 'overwalk', if it is allowed to run through the bridle. You should aim for a rhythmic, even, active, four-time beat with the pony using its hocks and shoulder. A good way of achieving this feel is to ride the pony down a hill.

The Trot

The trot is the pace which sorts the wheat from the chaff, and will either thrill or disappoint the judge with equal regularity; in my book it is the most important pace and if a pony really impresses at the trot you can forgive many other shortcomings. Nowadays you do not see so often the flat-out racing trot whereby the jockey, in the hope of impressing the judges, 'laps' the other competitors. This is just as well, as the judge doesn't want to see a horse with its hocks in the next county, falling on its forehand; this used to be called the Lancashire trot because a certain exhibitor trained his ponies this particular way! A pony with a naturally light, extravagant, balanced trot – like Holly of Spring – is a delight to watch; however, not all animals possess this gift. Steady, careful schooling can do much to improve a short irregular stride, and shoeing with aluminium plates will help a little. The trot in the hunter, show hunter pony and working hunter pony can be more workmanlike than that of the daintier hacks and show ponies.

The Canter

Very rarely do we see a beautifully balanced canter in the show ring; it is often too slow and stiff, especially in hack classes where many of the horses are going behind the movement. Although the hack canter is not supposed to be as forceful as the hunter canter – a morning canter in the park was not supposed to cover a lot of ground as one in the hunting field was – it should be smooth and elegant with a horse's hocks well engaged. It is surprising how many riders make a reasonable canter look worse because they are unable to sit in the saddle and absorb the movement, which is very off-putting for the judge. How often do you hear a judge, after dismounting, say that he was surprised with the good ride? Something must have given him the wrong impression in the first place!

The Gallop

The good gallop is the one that lowers and lengthens, and covers the ground, almost like putting a car into overdrive; it is certainly nothing to do with scuttling along and speed. If you want to learn how to gallop, just watch David Tatlow in operation – he manages to collect the horses going into the corner so that they come out balanced but fully extended. Too many children tag around the back of the line-up and then spring into action like a cavalry charge; then they come back to a slow canter immediately, giving the impression that there was a lot of fuss about nothing. A good gallop can win or lose a pony class and is an essential item in the repertoire of a hunter, a working hunter pony and a show hunter pony.

The show horse must learn to stand and maintain a halt at any time; and once you have achieved this, you can teach your horse to rein-back. Many attempts at the rein-back in the show ring are pathetic; either the rider pulls the animal's head off or the animal shuffles back half a stride giving the impression of being completely wooden. You must have your animal between hand and leg before you do anything; then, using both leg and hand, gently ask your animal to go back four even strides, then to go forward four even strides – without either bolting back or rushing forwards. When teaching a horse to back, especially a young one who may make a meal of it, it may be a good idea to try this in long reins from the ground first of all, or at least get an assistant to put his hand on the horse's chest and using the voice, ask him to back. At all times be patient; you may not get the required number of strides to begin with, but you must never, ever, resort to brute force.

A good gallop is achieved when the horse lowers and lengthens
. . . not *when he springs into action like a cavalry charger!*

PROBLEMS

In most cases good feeding, strapping and correct schooling will be enough for a show animal gradually to take shape and come together. It is common sense, however, that if certain problems or weaknesses exist, then extra work and thought are required to eradicate and improve them. For instance, concentrated uphill work will be beneficial to those animals which are weak or idle behind because it will make them use their hindlegs more than they would on the flat. Similarly, downhill work will encourage the poor walker to use his shoulder blades more. If a horse is ewe-necked because he works above the bit all the time, it may be necessary to use draw reins to encourage him – but not to force him – to lower his head carriage and flex at the poll. This will eventually improve the top line.

Once an older pony has developed a habit, it takes a little longer to rectify and a great deal of patience. We once had a 14.2hh pony which had a habit of striking off on the wrong leg; initially this was because the animal needed his back checking and because he was not supple enough – for instance, he always went on the wrong bend. However, even when these problems had been dealt with, he would still have a tendency to do it. The solution to this was to canter him across a slope which encouraged him to take off on the required (uphill) leg – otherwise he would have lost his balance. Sometimes it pays to experiment and get to the root of a problem by eliminating all possible causes.

One problem which requires a great deal of time and patience is when a horse will not stand still, either when mounting and dismounting, or after a show, or even in a line-up. Your only hope of rectifying this problem is to keep somebody on the horse for as long, and for as many times as possible – if necessary have your breakfast, lunch and dinner on top of him, and hopefully he will eventually come to terms with the idea. Have an assistant at hand to reward him from time to time, just as you would when mounting and dismounting, and you will reap the benefit in the long run. Some people make a horse face a wall when they mount or dismount, with an assistant at the horse's head to talk to him and stop him from shooting backwards. With problems of this sort, you almost have to brainwash the animal so as to make the bad habit good.

The author riding Layton Ambassador up a hill. This work is excellent for encouraging a horse to use his hindlegs

A horse which naps when leaving either the stable yard or another animal in the school or on a lorry, needs sorting out straightaway: send him firmly forwards, if necessary using spurs and a whip. If not corrected immediately this problem may manifest itself in the ring, when the horse will either refuse to leave the line-up or will nap towards the entrance. Similarly, if an animal has a dislike of certain objects in the ring – such as flags, show jumps or umbrellas – try and put some up in the schooling area so that they become an everyday occurrence.

We have the radio on in the stable yard most of the time as we believe that this accustoms the show animals to noise in the show ring. We are also lucky to live near an aerodrome so that planes occasionally fly overhead either after taking off or before landing – the ponies therefore get quite used to the noise. It is surprising how many showgrounds are near an airfield and how many ponies 'boil' when hearing a jet engine.

One of the most important points to remember when schooling is to keep the work programme interesting, even if you are concentrating on something like circles – change the rein often, do serpentines; when schooling in general, pop over the odd jump or do some cavaletti work. A bored horse is more likely to develop vices and bad manners than a happy one, and once a show horse has lost interest in life it takes a clever producer to nurse it back.

THE CHILD RIDER

When producing an animal that is to be ridden by a judge, make sure that it will behave for anyone, regardless of the ability, size or weight of the rider! Because of this, it is often thought that producing hacks and hunters is far more demanding than children's ponies. However, training children is just as difficult a job and is an art in itself.

A Good Jockey

At the end of the day, a good jockey can be the all-deciding factor and his riding will decide whether your show animal is going to be a champion or a flop. If you put an experienced jockey on a green pony or a 'kidder', more often than not it will beat a very high class exhibit which is badly ridden. A show horse has been described as a musical instrument and the jockey as the musician: it is possible for a jockey to cover up a multitude of badly tuned faults when showing. In pony classes this cover can be maintained, unlike the horse classes when the judge has to be able to get a good tune out of the exhibit too. This is often the reason for the top riders 'nagging' the horses whilst they are still in the ring and before being ridden by the judge, in the hope that the magic will last a little longer.

Showmanship

Ronnie Marmont once said that showing off was the name of the game and that every good jockey must have a sense of theatre; just as we look for presence in the show animal, so flair is essential in the top show jockey, whether natural or cultivated. The rider must be noticed but only for the right reasons – not because he is bumping up and down in the saddle – nor should he over-do the showmanship lest he defeats his object and overshadows the horse!

Without doubt, showing can give the junior rider a good grounding at an impressionable early age – some who were excellent child riders are still with us today, many of them producing horses themselves or judging at the top shows, and there are many who have gone into other equestrian fields and are equally successful: Jennie Loriston-Clarke who rode, amongst others, Royal Show, the only pony who ever beat Pretty Polly, and who is Britain's leading dressage rider; her sister Jane Holderness–Roddam, an international horse trials rider; in show jumping there is Ted Edgar, who rode Debutante; and Jane Thelwall who won Burghley Horse Trials in 1988, and who as Jane Soutar rode Favourita to win Pony of the Year at Wembley in 1967; and many more . . .!

Better Standards

Even though you may still see some awful sights, the general standard of riding nowadays has improved, as has the overall quality of ponies. Parents are more aware of presentation, and often take the opportunity of booking their jockeys into some of the excellent teaching courses run by the area branches of the BSPS and Ponies UK around the country. They realise that children will often listen to 'outside' people more than mum and dad, who anyway quite often don't ride themselves – although in fact it does not follow that you have to be a good rider yourself in order to be a good teacher.

Tuition

If jockeys are to benefit from any type of tuition, there must be a set plan beforehand: treat tuition like a jigsaw, take out one piece at a time and discuss it – whether it be leg positions one week, or in-hand shows the next – as long as these pieces are joined together at some point to complete the overall picture. With smaller jockeys the main thing is to keep everything clear and simple, and above all enjoyable. Keep the subject matter very light, by using cones or making out figures of eight with chalk lines. At this age, it is helpful to keep your subject visual so the child can see what is required. At the other end of the scale, the older jockeys need to be taught on a more individual, discursive basis – after years of being told to ride with an inside bend, or to aim for a short stride when approaching a fence, there comes a point when they want to know *why* they should be asking for these actions. Instead of just being passengers, they want to learn to feel for a horse but want this feel now backed by sound knowledge. Some jockeys, just like some animals, have natural ability but even these lucky few should be able to understand the theory behind the job. Jockeys who may not be as talented but have the intelligence to understand and put this into practice will also succeed.

Learning to Ride

Even though enjoyment is the key to it all, showing is becoming more professional each year and to be successful you must keep up with the high standards demanded. Jockeys can often be seen not sitting up straight in the saddle, and looking down all the time instead of looking ahead – if you can teach a child to look up and think forwards the animal will go forwards; if he is looking down all the time, the horse will appear to be on the forehand and behind the movement. Some perform minor acrobatics when asking for canter, tipping forwards or dropping the inside shoulder – presumably to check if they are on the correct lead; it

13.2hh show pony Cusop Heiress: three times Champion at Royal Windsor and beautifully produced by the Gilbert-Scott family. It was a shame she came out at the same time as the legendary Holly of Spring, whom she beat just once

A pony type of 14.2hh: Oakley Bubbling Patrick, Champion at the Three Counties Show

is more likely they will be on the wrong one because they have shifted their weight out of the saddle at a crucial moment.

Some jockeys do find downward transitions difficult, especially from gallop, and from canter to trot; they will often adopt a sort of water-skiing position because they are getting left behind, which is very unsightly. Riding in a straight-cut, soup-plate showing saddle is difficult enough for a show rider with a well developed seat; if your inexperienced jockey does tend to get left behind, make him more secure by using a dressage-style show saddle with knee rolls. If your jockey rises up and down too high at trot and is still being left behind, this could be because he is riding with too long a stirrup.

Hands

It is imperative that a jockey is taught to have sympathetic hands – bad hands can ruin a pony's mouth in such a short time. He must keep them individual, so that he can use one independently of the other (as with the legs), and must keep them in front of the saddle rather than at chin level or at the pony's elbow. From a side-view, the back of each hand should be obvious, with the thumbs on top as if carrying two tumblers of water, and elbows at the rider's side – not, as sometimes seen, the 'knitting position' with the wrists rounded. By keeping his elbows in at the side and his thumbs pressing onto the reins, the child has a better chance of keeping hold of the reins and maintaining a consistent steady contact.

If a jockey has trouble with loopy reins, it may be advisable to knot them at suitable intervals to stop them slipping through his fingers – though this wouldn't happen if they were held between the thumb and first finger. On wet show days those gloves with rubber stipples on the palm are best for keeping hold of wet, slippery reins.

You can always tell if a hand is coming out of play by the way the stick is held: correctly, on the right rein the schooling whip, held in the inside hand, should lie at a south-west angle against the jockey's thigh; however, if the wrists are rounded with the elbows sticking out like a goose, the whip will take more of a

A more horsey type of 14.2hh show pony: Touchdown, Champion at the Devon County Show, and a winner at Wembley in 1981

The trot sorts the wheat from the chaff! Brewster, Lightweight Show Hunter of the Year, 1982

(Above) Teach a child to think forwards, and the horse will go forwards

(Right) Jockeys sometimes perform minor acrobatics. Notice that the reins are too long and dangerous

(Far Right) Jockeys must be taught to have sympathetic hands; bad hands can ruin a pony's mouth

westerly line – and if the hands are held into the chest, then the stick will lie in a southern tilt. This usually happens because the jockey has his reins too long, and instead of being able to take a good contact and give with his hands in a forwards direction, he is trying to shorten them by drawing them towards the body, and consequently is taking rather than giving.

The Correct Diagonal

It is essential that jockeys are taught to ride on the correct diagonal at the trot, because if an animal is ridden on the wrong one it can look unbalanced or even lame. At rising trot, the rider should be sitting in the saddle when the outside foreleg and the inside hindleg are touching the ground. If the jockey cannot tell the difference from on board, tell him to watch the outside shoulder blade; from the ground it is better to watch the inside hindleg. No matter who the jockey is, the general riding position will need polishing every so often, otherwise bad habits develop – a good way is to have a lunge lesson without stirrups.

If you have a particular problem with your horse relating to its individual show or in the ring – for example, it may be not turning soon enough into the change of rein – take this out of your programme and concentrate on it, rather than practising the show in full every time, just as dressage riders do when a particular section of a test needs more polish. Many young jockeys become very anxious when doing their individual display in the ring, and freeze as if they had been asked to do the impossible. There is no reason for this: an individual show is simply a series of movements which a rider performs anyway in his every-day riding.

If your animal is well schooled and you are capable of producing a good performance, this will go a long way towards persuading the judge to have you at the top end of the line-up. You may not be able to alter a horse's basic conformation but you can do much to improve and alter his way of going – one is bestowed by God, the other is largely man-made.

CHAPTER 5

Preparation for the Show

TRIMMING

During the winter months, quite a bit of trimming can be done to improve appearances for the following summer. Tails which have become very thin over the previous summer, probably with too much brushing, can be banged quite short to encourage the hair to grow (and to keep them out of the mud); unruly manes can be encouraged to grow over to the off-side by regular water brushing, or by plaiting over and holding in place with elastic bands.

Sometimes animals arrive in our yard early in the spring already trimmed out. In many cases, too much top-knot has been cut out, or too much wither hair clipped off, and not very much can be done about this actually during the show season, unless you allow the hair to grow again which can look an untidy mess. Winter is a good time to allow these parts of the mane to grow, likewise any thin spots, and coconut oil rubbed into the skin will aid hair growth. Similarly, if a tail has been razored during the show season, let this grow out during the winter so that it can be pulled the following spring, as there is nothing nicer than a well pulled tail in the ring. Some producers can razor a tail so well during the summer show season that it is very difficult to distinguish from a pulled tail. However, more often than not a razored tail can be spotted a mile off in the show ring and is often a horrific sight.

Tail-pulling

Pulling tails is an art in itself and your top-class show animal is not the one to practise on. Most animals will not object if only a few hairs at a time are taken out, rather than a handful in one fell swoop. The best time is when a pony or horse comes in from exercise warm, when the pores are open. Hair texture varies from one animal to another – sometimes it falls out at the merest tug, with others it is like wire wool; this is the worst sort, as it has an elastic property which makes it difficult to pull out and it does

89

not lie flat afterwards. The use of rubber gloves will help the handler get a better and more accurate grip, and if the animal is likely to kick whilst the job is being done, stand behind a straw bale – even better, hang the tail over a door so that the tail-pulling is being done on the outside and the pony is kicking the door rather than your legs!

Remove the side hairs to give the tail a fluted look and take excess bushy hair from on top so that the hair lies flat along the dock. Some docks are thicker and longer than others, so it is important to examine how a pony carries its tail so that you can see how far down the dock to go. If the tail is bandaged every day this will train the hair to lie flat and give you an idea how the shape of the pulled tail is progressing. However, never put the bandage on too tight or for too long (ie overnight) as this will make the underside of the tail sore and sometimes results in the hair being killed altogether, leaving bald patches. It is better to dampen the hair with a water brush rather than wet the tail bandage, as the bandage will tighten as it dries and be difficult to pull off. If there are signs of blood when pulling a tail, wash with lukewarm water and mild antiseptic to guard against infection.

The overall picture one is trying to create is, from the side, a well-rounded arc; and from the back, one of symmetry – with thicker tails it may be necessary to thin hair further down the tail as a thick, bushy tail will give the impression of cobbiness and lack of quality. The length of a tail is very important, and the general rule is to have it level with the hocks when it is carried; have an assistant to hold it in its natural carriage position whilst you level the tail at the required length with the clippers (scissors can easily leave 'steps'). Many people bang the tail when it is in its resting position so that when the pony moves off and cocks his tail, the end slopes at about 45°; it is also easy to make the mistake of taking too much off the tail, which if it has a high carriage anyway, could look disastrous!

Tails that are too long can exaggerate a low-set tail-carriage, whereas a tail at the correct length can improve the look of the hind leg and emphasise a neat outline. Show cobs usually have tails a little shorter than other riding horses to create that cobby

With the help of an assistant, trim the bottom of the tail so that it is level (Inset) The use of rubber gloves will allow the handler a better grip when pulling a tail. Hang the tail over the stable door if the pony is likely to kick

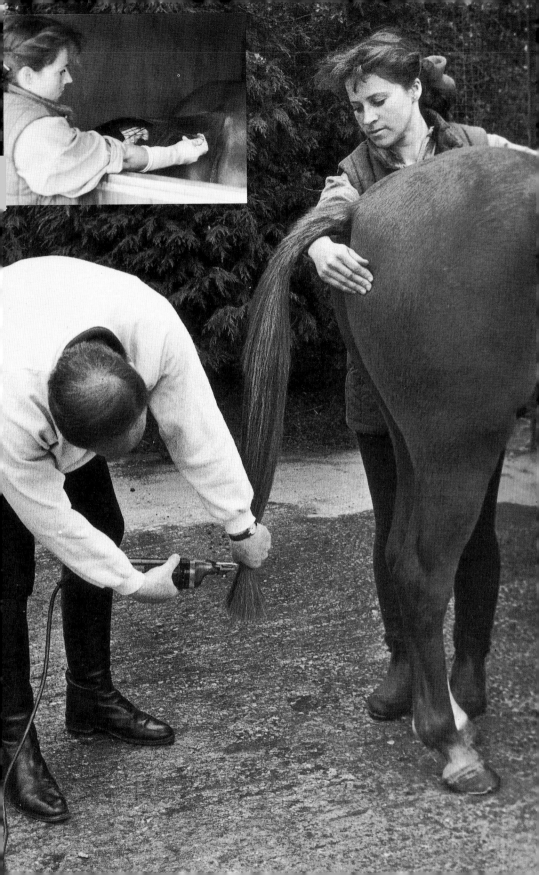

'sumo wrestler' look; and ponies with long backs look better for having shorter tails as long tails make them look as if they go on for ever. Judges are not stupid, either, and will not overlook faulty hocks and hind action because they are hidden by long bushy tails. A thin tail must be well looked after; it can be braided the day before a show as when unravelled, the resulting waviness can give the appearance of more depth – just as a perm is supposed to give a head of hair more body.

Manes

We allow manes to grow as much as possible during the winter months, and even snip the ends of thin areas as soon as the animals are roughed off in the hope that this will create an even length of mane by springtime. At the intermediate stage of growth, which coincides with the first pulling of the season, the mane near the wither is usually left altogether as this is the part often rubbed by rugs, and nearer showing time if pulled is often lost which can look unsightly. When pulling the mane to plaiting length, try to keep it an even length and thickness; any thin areas can be levelled with scissors, as pulling will only make these even thinner – if the mane is of different thicknesses, this will show in the plaits which will also be of different sizes. Animals with a thick crest and wide hair growth are the most difficult to pull, as it is often desirable to get the mane short so that small plaits can be made, but at the same time the mane needs to be thin which means taking more from underneath.

Preparing the mane before plaiting is just as important as cleaning an animal properly before putting on the show gloss and the hoof oil.

Trimming when Rough

When animals come in at the beginning of the season to start work, they are trimmed to keep them tidy but not to the degree that they would be for the ring – for instance, ears are just levelled off rather than taken out; feathers are removed from legs, although the hair from the heels is not completely trimmed so as to give protection from mud fever if the pony is still being turned out; and top-knots are only taken out a little bit so that mane is not trapped under the head-piece of the bridle.

The mane: When preparing for the show ring, careful consideration should be made when trimming – done incorrectly, and the picture which you are trying to create can easily look all wrong.

One of the most common mistakes is to be too ambitious with a pair of scissors or clippers, and to take out too much top-knot or too much wither hair which loses valuable plaiting space. This is particularly disadvantageous if the animal is short of front, when it will need as many plaits as possible. Likewise if too much mane is clipped from the poll region, it can leave the forelock hair very thin and will particularly emphasise the jaw of an animal, sometimes making it look very 'Arab-like', or plain in the head. In the case of a grey, if the pony's head is a slightly different shade to the rest of its body do not cut too much out, otherwise it will look as if the head belongs to a different animal. In general, 1 to 1½in is enough, just so there is room for the head-piece of the bridle. If the forelock is insufficient, you may have to leave the top-knot altogether and use it to supplement the forelock hair.

If a pony lacks wither, clip off some of the mane but without going too far up the neck – this should help to give it one. Exposing the point of the wither will normally give more emphasis to the shoulder and improve the general topline altogether, unless your animal is desperately short of front – the mane in this region is usually thin and dead anyway, so it is impossible to get a decent plait. Just as it is bad practice to take away too much plaiting area, it is equally unsightly to plait beyond the wither so that the plaits disappear under the saddle, although this is more acceptable in an in-hand class.

The legs: Be careful when trimming legs out – ponies which are light of bone should not have the clippers run down the backs of their legs, as this will emphasise the fault. Likewise ponies which are long in the pastern do not want the heels clipped so short as to look skinned, as this will make the pastern look longer than ever. If your animal clips a different colour, be careful not to go too high up the legs or it will appear to be tied in below the knee; worse still, clipping will leave a curb-line just below the hock. We always trim out the heels with clippers (not a comb and scissors), without making them look skinned, and only trim down the back of the leg if the limb appears common and has untidy hair.

The head: Trimming out in the spring is a lot more difficult than in midsummer, as 'lines' can easily be left when clipping into dead winter coat which is a lot thicker than the baby hair of a summer coat. This is a particular problem when trimming the head, especially when confronted with teething bumps and narrow jaw bones! When trimming under the head, the trick is to have a clean, level line; do not come up too far above the underside of the jaw-bone which will leave a ragged line, and be careful how much hair you take out around the throat region. When taking off whiskers around the muzzle and eyes, we use a disposable razor which does a good job – not, as you sometimes see, whiskers half-removed and mixed with ½in of stubble, which looks worse than keeping the full whiskers on! Unless the animal is a bit of a head shaker, we always trim the ears out fully, and find that small hand clippers are very useful for this operation.

At Blue Slate we are fanatical about trimming, and even if an animal takes a dislike to the clippers we ask the vet to sedate him for a short time whilst the exercise is completed. Make sure that you allow sufficient time for the tranquiliser to leave the animal's system just in case you are subjected to a random dope test at a show. Trimming gives a neater outline even to a pretty animal, so it follows that a plainer one can be improved even more.

CLIPPING

If you are working your show animal during the winter months or are showing on the winter circuit, you may consider removing more of the coat than normal, or even clipping out fully; this is something we usually do for Wembley if woolly coats spoil the outline, and have even done in summer, especially with grey ponies which have lost their dapples. We find that clipping out fully can make greys a better colour – the dapples return – and give them more quality, allowing them to compete more favourably against their shiny bay and brown counterparts.

When clipping, the golden rule is to clip according to the amount of work which is going to be done, and to how much time the animal is going to spend outside in the field. If an animal is prone to sweating and is in hard work, remove more hair than if it is doing only weekend work and living outside most of the time. Chills can be caught just as easily by sweating too much, as standing around in the cold for too long.

From a showing point of view, various types of clip can help cover up conformation faults. For instance, if an animal is short of bone and is competing in WHP and SHP classes during the winter months, give him a hunter clip which is very much in keeping with the nature of the class and more importantly, will allow the legs to remain hairy thus giving the appearance of having more bone. Clipping above the muscle line at the top of the leg can make a leggy animal more butty, and below the line will have the opposite effect. The size and shape of the saddle patch can also be used, either to 'fill up' a long-backed pony or to give a short-coupled pony more scope and create a picture of having more depth. Similarly a bib clip can make a stuffy front look cleaner, a trace clip will give a very short-coupled pony the appearance of having more scope, and a blanket clip will shorten a long-backed pony. Even though the animal is still the same underneath, you are trying to deceive the judges for the few seconds they have when battling against a gruelling timetable.

Whichever clip you choose, make sure that it is the same and even on both sides otherwise it may look as though an animal has a dropped hip or something. If you do not possess the essential eagle eye for symmetry, chalk out areas and use a piece of string to measure out more accurately. When doing lines try to be accurate first time for best results.

Before you start clipping, make sure that your animal is well groomed so that the clippers are not overworked and will clip efficiently. Have a soft brush and some light oil at hand for the same reason – it is the overworked clippers which soon get hot. We use fine blades which are sharpened regularly and without fail have a full set of teeth; it is the blades with broken teeth which cause the nicks in the soft folds of skin. Run the clippers for a while so that the animal becomes accustomed to the noise, and when starting remember to keep the clippers flat against the skin, drawing them backwards and forwards smoothly, rather than at an angle to the coat in a digging manner. We always start under the belly and work up to the shoulder region, just in case the animal takes fright and this has to be altered to a sweat clip, continuing up the neck and head if all is well. When doing difficult areas such as the belly and elbows, the clippers will run better if the loose skin is more stretched – do this either by using your hand or getting an assistant to pull a leg forward. On a cold day give the animal a good groom and strapping; otherwise give him a warm bath to get rid of the excess grease. Make sure that he is kept warm afterwards, even if this means putting on stable bandages for a couple of days.

No matter how proficient you are at clipping, and it is something that comes with practice, if the animal is in poor condition it will look in a sorry state. On the other hand, the animal which is healthy and bonny-looking will shortly afterwards look a million dollars. Boiled feeds will go a long way to keeping him warm and consequently his coat will shine like glass.

WASHING

As many of our inmates go out in the field the day before a show, they generally require a bath when they come in, even though they are well groomed each day. Those ponies which tend to keep themselves spotless sometimes go without, but the grey ponies without exception do not, unless the weather is particularly cold and a pony's coat tends to suffer through excessive bathing – then an extra grooming is given instead. It is important to note that all pulling and trimming is done prior to bathing, except for checking the level of the tail with a pair of scissors.

Make sure that all the water buckets, brushes, sponges, shampoo, towels, sweat-scraper, anti-sweat rugs and bandages are at hand *before* you attempt to give the bath; it is surprising how many people tie the animal up without a rug and sometimes on a cold day, and only then proceed to collect all the items. Always use a good shampoo and if possible put this in the water as well – quite often the pony gets covered in soap suds because the shampoo has been too liberally applied to its coat, and it therefore takes a long time to rinse it off completely. We usually have two soapy water buckets with a sponge and water brush, with double the amount of rinsing buckets and a fresh rinsing sponge to go with them.

We have found that it is far easier to do the head completely first of all, drying it off as well; and make sure that the headcollar (a Cottage Craft type one is better than leather for this job) is clean before it goes back on the head, otherwise your clean animal will be left with a grubby mark where the dirty headcollar has been. You can then proceed with the rest of the body, without having to worry about soap getting into the horse's eyes and ears. It is important when washing the mane and tail that they are cleaned right down to the roots, and also that particular attention is paid to white socks. Before rinsing, use the last of the soapy water to wash the feet – although I have seen people bath a horse and leave it with muddy hooves! On warm days we use a hose-pipe to rinse off all the excess soap, and then warmer water to give a final rinse.

Many people do not rinse the animal well enough, especially around the mane region and do not therefore get that squeaky-clean effect which you will when it is done well. Sometimes it is necessary to put extras in the rinsing water to get a better result. For instance: a couple of capfuls of white vinegar will help to tone the skin and is especially good after clipping, lifting out any lines.

About the same amount of fabric conditioner helps to reduce the static in dark-coated animals which attracts dust – we once had a black pony with a super coat and every time we gave it a rub over with a cloth it became very dusty until we used conditioner in the rinsing water. The grey ponies, especially with grey manes and tails, are rinsed with optical bleach in the water to get the blue-white effect which so many of the soap powder commercials boast about. With yellow-grey tails, we have sometimes used a platinum-rinse shampoo which has worked with great success.

Using a sweat-scraper and towels, dry the animal off well – it is essential that it is dry before it is put back into the stable, even if this entails a walk or a quick lunge. Some animals will roll immediately they return to the stable, and these are usually tied up for a while so they dry off completely. It is a good idea after bathing to put a clean cotton sheet next to the pony's skin, to keep it clean. Grey tails can be kept clean in a stocking held under a tail bandage. White socks can be bandaged once the ceiling-white paste or shoe whitener has dried. We have been known to cover grey ponies all over in talcum powder or in a weak solution of ceiling-white paste before rugging up; this was brushed out at the show the next morning.

A grey pony does need that extra bit of attention: when it seems almost luminous it looks good; if it has a yellow cast to its colour, it looks awful.

TACK AND CLOTHING

Once your show animal is trimmed and bathed in preparation for the next day's show you can concentrate on other jobs such as tack cleaning, packing the horsebox and getting the horses' rugs and bandages ready. This saves rushing around on a show morning when there will be enough to do as it is. All the tack, including any exercise tack going to the show, is cleaned the day before so that it only needs a quick wipe over on show day – those people lucky enough to have two sets of tack can put a clean set on the pony minutes before going into the ring. To take ponies into the ring and show them with dirty tack is a nonsense when so much time and effort has been spent on turning yourself and the horse out to a high standard, and is also an insult to the judge. You have only to look at the state of some of the ride-judges' jodhpurs to see that this is not an uncommon situation.

Tack

Tack will remain supple if oiled and saddle-soaped regularly. However, a common problem when saddle-soaping is that the sponge gets too wet and too soapy, so that deposits are left on the tack and clog up the holes on the bridle which looks messy. Similarly, when oiling tack, do not drown the leather-work otherwise for the next few months holding the reins will be like ringing out a wet dishcloth, and they will be too slippery to hold.

When cleaning bits with metal polish make sure that the mouth-piece is washed afterwards so that the ponies cannot taste the polish. A good way to get a shine on metal and an easy way to shine metal curb chains, is to rub them up with a handful of bran.

When cleaning tack, make a note of which holes are used on each bridle, so that everything is put together again correctly – it may have taken you some time to get the bit at the right height in the pony's mouth, and the show ring is not the place to discover that the bridle has been adjusted. Likewise stitching – the tackroom, the day before a show, is the place to check for any loose stitching, whilst cleaning the tack.

Make sure that the stirrups will be big enough for the ride-judge and that stirrup leathers will adjust enough to cater for various leg lengths. We always have a permanent selection of girths and numnahs in the horsebox, together with some lungeing tack and a hole-punch as well, in case it is necessary to make any final alterations. Once the tack has been cleaned and carefully checked over it is moved to the horsebox en bloc, and up to date we have rarely arrived at a show with the wrong tack.

Accessories

Coloured browbands are made at home and all the animals are shown in the stable colours which most of the time are red, white and blue, in the hope that the rosettes will be a perfect match! When dirty, these usually come clean when steamed over a kettle; one lady uses washable plastic browbands covered in velvet ribbon and has put them in the washing machine time and time again with great success – a leather browband would turn the velvet brown.

Most owners have great fun co-ordinating browband colours with those of the shirts, ties, hair ribbons and button holes; sometimes these are rather over the top, but they usually enhance the picture. Make sure that your browband is of a suitable width to match the size of the animal. For instance, a lead-rein pony will need a narrow one whereas a wider one would suit a horse, and the latter can have wider triangles made from a wider velvet ribbon. The cross-looking pony with his bridle almost slipping off because the browband is too tight is a sorry sight; and by the same token there is no excuse for having a browband which droops between the eyes like a tiara!

Travelling Clothes

All our animals have separate travelling clothes which are bought as a set and look very smart; these consist of a leather headcollar (sometimes with the pony's name on a brass plate), rope, anti-sweat rug, summer sheet, woollen day rug, show roller, tail bandage, tail guard, leg bandages, and foam pads which mould to the shape of the leg to cover hocks and knees – these save having to put on hock and knee boots. Not being a fan of chains, we use tarred ropes if the animal has a tendency to chew things. It is important that the clip always fastens away from the muzzle – I have seen the clip lodged in the narrow jaw line when fastened the other way.

It is important that the clip always fastens away from the muzzle

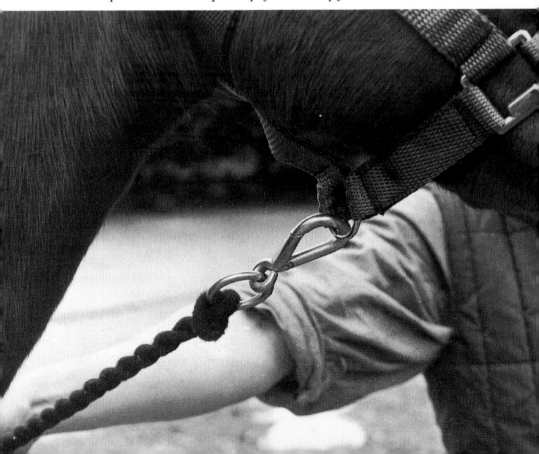

The darker-coloured foam pads for the legs keep a lot cleaner than the white ones. We only use the fur pads with velcro fastenings as an alternative to bandages when going short distances – to the beach or the indoor school; knee boots and hock boots are only used if the particular animal scrapes in front or sits on his hocks when travelling, but knee boots are always worn when hacking out. These are very often put on badly, either too slack so they slip as soon as the animal moves, or too tight so they cause swelling – not recommended when arriving at a show! The top straps should be fastened securely, the bottom ones quite loosely. Rather than put these on wrongly, it may be better to use the full-length hock protector pads instead.

When putting on stable and travelling bandages, let the gamgee meet and start the bandage on the inside or outside of the leg, *not* at the back of the tendons. Otherwise the back of the leg may be aggravated, just as a piece of straw trapped under the gamgee may cause a reaction. For the same reason, fasten the tapes of the bandage on the inside or outside rather than on the front or the back of the leg.

Bandages which are too short are exasperating, so when buying for horses make sure that they are longer than the normal pony size. Always start about mid-way down the leg and work downwards, remembering to cover and protect the fetlock region, then proceed to bandage up the leg keeping the pressure firm rather than tight and the bandage evenly spaced on the leg. Finish just above the starting point and fasten the tapes securely (the velcro fastenings are good), tucking them into the bandage.

Obviously on a hot day the animals may only need a cotton sheet to travel in, and some will only need a sweat sheet if they have a tendency to break out when travelling long distances. The temperature can vary so much during the summer season, from the chill when setting off at the crack of dawn to the heat of a mid-day heat-wave, and it is up to the people travelling with the animals to make sure that they are comfortable en route; this very often means adjusting rugs and opening windows and sky-lights for more ventilation.

TRAVEL

The Journey

It is important to look after show animals whilst travelling: make sure that they have a hay net to munch at, sufficient to drink, that they are not too hot or too cold and that they have enough space in the partitions; they will then arrive at the show relaxed and in good shape. Some people cram their animals into tight partitions, including mares and foals, and never check them at all until they arrive on the show ground after a journey made in record-breaking time. They then wonder why the animals are run up and wet through, with bandages and rugs hanging off.

The Horsebox

Even though our box floor has rubber matting, we still bed it down with either shavings or straw because it can become very slippery when wet. It is important to learn how much room your animal prefers when travelling – some like to be fairly tight, whilst others spread their hindlegs apart and will fall over if too enclosed. Once an animal has had a bad experience in a horsebox, it will take a long time to regain its confidence, and it will have to be travelled with a great deal of care – after all, what use is a show animal if it will not travel to a show?

On a very long journey it may be necessary to give the animals a rest, and they can then perhaps have a small feed; although when returning from a long day on a showfield, I actually like to get our animals in their own stables as quickly as possible – but not at break-neck speed.

Breakdowns

One year we were returning from the RIHS with a cob when we broke down on the side of the motorway; we didn't arrive home until seven the next morning and as a result the cob nearly died of exhaustion and stress. We have therefore become members of a road rescue service which guarantees immediate breakdown recovery, and also provides stabling and accommodation if necessary. This sort of cover is essential if travelling all around the country with show animals, and is well worth the nominal fee.

Other Essentials

With all the various items of tack already mentioned, including spare bits and curb chains, the horsebox sometimes resembles a travelling tack shop; there are, moreover, other important items which should be on the check-list. These include a veterinary kit, a first-aid kit, and a box file with all the appropriate passes and schedules as well as height certificates, registration certificates and flu cards. It is also advisable to take spare rugs and bandages, headcollars and ropes (you are stuck if a headcollar breaks, as the animal should not travel home in a bridle), show rugs and sheets for the show ring, and waterproof rugs (all with fillet strings in case it is a windy day), grooming kit, washing stuff, a box for show days containing hoof oil, tack cleaning stuff and so on – and most important, horse food and portable mangers even if you are not stopping overnight. An overnight stay will mean that additional hay, bedding, mucking-out equipment, tarpaulin covers for the stables and padlocks must all be added to the check-list.

Loading

During the show season the horsebox is a combination of mobile home and working stable yard, quite apart from being a transport vehicle too! Some of the boxes to be seen on the show grounds are the height of luxury, yet this is sometimes at the expense of the horse and the workmanship in the horse department is shoddy, with flimsy, cramped partitions and so on. The horsebox may look very fancy with all its stripes, but if it rocks from side to side around every corner and gives a very bad ride, it is not surprising if the horse doesn't want to go in. Of the bad loaders, the ones who are not frightened (but are just trying it on) will often soon give up, and in the end have been the quickest loaders in the yard, but more patience is needed with the animals who are genuinely frightened; and careful driving will help them over-come their fear once they are on board the lorry – generally, practice makes perfect.

Many a time a horse will not load because the box looks very dark and dismal inside – we had a box which was white inside, and nearly every animal was happy to go in. Similarly with a front-unload trailer, an animal will often load better if the side ramp is down, letting in more light. Any box will look more inviting if it is bedded down with straw, and if the ramp has side gates there is less chance of the animal coming off the side and hurting itself, and frightening itself further. By enclosing the loading area by the ramp, you are also reducing the number of escape routes to a bare minimum.

If the animal is the type who gets half inside the box and then rears up, it is advisable to use a poll guard or make one with a stable rubber or small piece of foam. If you are loading by yourself – which is a great disadvantage – you can attach a lunge rein to a gate post or the ramp gate to give yourself an extra pair of hands.

Whichever method you adopt, whether a small feed, straw on the ramp or literally manhandling the pony into the box, it is better to practise at home well before a show, rather than having to discover this problem on a show day. It must be soul-destroying to struggle all day at a show with a bad loader, and despite a crowd of experts, to no avail – to be still there, tired and exhausted, when people are going home at the end of the day.

CHAPTER 6

The Morning of the Show

TRAVEL

We usually prefer to travel to a show through the night rather than stable overnight on the showground, and there are quite a few reasons for doing this; the day before the show can then be a full working day at home, besides which the temporary boxes at most shows are simply inadequate in bad weather – many people will remember a few years ago at Wembley when most of the stables were flooded, some up to the horses' knees, and that was on a hard standing, not grass! Also, unless you can park your lorry next to the showground stabling, your animals are left unattended, which is not a good thing when they can be subjected to random dope tests at the bigger shows. And the general public always offers quite unsuitable things like toffees, or cups of tea to stabled horses, quite apart from the fact that they never give the animals a moment's peace. It is therefore much better to have them within the quieter, more secure confines of your horsebox.

Overnight Arrangements

If we do have to stay overnight, because we are competing on more than one day at a show, or because a particular animal benefits from resting after a long journey, we usually stable with friends en route, returning this favour if ever they show in our area. The exception to this is at Wembley where it is better to stable on the ground rather than risk getting stuck in peak-hour traffic when journeying from stabling out of town.

Because we choose to travel through the night or on the morning of the show, we have to start work in the early hours in order to allow ourselves enough time to give the animals a feed, a quick groom (or even another bath if one is a grey) and to put on bandages before travelling. It is always better to get up that little bit earlier and set off for a show in good time, than to end up rushing about and hoping that everything will remain composed in the ring.

Preparations before Departure

With classes at some shows starting at 8am, it is sometimes advisable to do even more preparatory work before you set off. This could entail a quick lunge before a feed or plaiting up the pony before leaving, so that once on the show field you have enough time to work him in properly and get him polished off for the ring.

If we are setting off for a show very early in the morning, the really naughty ponies who are living out are brought in at teatime the day before, trimmed and then bathed. Later they are plaited and tied up all night so they cannot lie down and have a sleep, in the hope that they will be relaxed and well-mannered at the show. Many people believe that travelling through the night can also take the edge off a naughty pony.

Our ponies are not usually untied in the stable once they have been plaited as they could get straw, shavings and other bits in the plaits and the hair may break, making the plaits look 'sprutty' if they are allowed to stretch their necks. Once an animal has finished his classes on show day however, the plaits are taken out there and then, even if showing again the next day. If a mane is to last all season, it must be cared for and after several hours animals may try to rub out their plaits and can easily remove whole clumps of the mane.

A loose cover can be secured over each plait with an elastic band

Normally when plaiting a pony before a show, it is advisable to leave the last two or three bottom plaits until after the animal has been worked in so that they cannot be disturbed by reins or neck–strap or the rider's hands. Hair spray and setting gel can be applied to plaits to help them keep their shape, especially the high, loose type. Sometimes plaits put in at, say, 11pm are expected to be just as good for a championship at 4pm the following day, which takes some doing! Some people who plait up the night before put on a hood or a loose cover for protection, secured over each plait with elastic bands.

PLAITING A MANE

Plaiting is an art in itself; done well, and a weak topline can be improved beyond all recognition, done badly and faults may be not only revealed, but exaggerated. It is surprising how different an animal can look once flowing hair disappears; it can become quite another shape, just as a girl with long hair can look quite different when her hair is up. Like people's hair, manes also vary from one pony to the next. Some hair is very easy to plait, and locks well and is easy to build up into a decent high plait; other manes are wiry and the hair has a mind of its own which always creates a lop-sided plait. This wiry type is improved by shampooing with conditioner to make it more manageable. Manes are often best washed two days before plaiting as some will stand on end when washed the day before, like a plume. Always make sure that a mane is rinsed well otherwise the hair is very slippery and difficult to plait, as well as creating an unsightly problem with dandruff.

Plaits should be neat and individually constructed, the three portions of hair divided in a clean-cut manner by using the end of a mane comb so that hair is not gathered from parts of another plait; wetting the mane well will make unruly hair easier to manipulate. If a mane is of even length and even thickness and the amount used for each plait is roughly the same, each one should look as though it belongs to the others; to help gauge the correct amount of mane, put an elastic band in the mane comb. If any part of the mane is thicker than the rest, this will show in the plaiting. Another common mistake is to spend too little time stitching the plait securely in the final stages, especially with loose, high plaits which sometimes wobble when the animal is moving or start to fall out with a sudden movement such as coughing.

An elastic band in the mane comb can be used to gauge the correct amount of mane

Plaiting to Improve Conformation

The general rule is that the more plaits you make, the longer the length of neck will appear; so that if an animal is short of front you want to do as many plaits as possible. Occasionally you may want to create the opposite picture; for instance, if a show animal resembles a giraffe and is out of proportion, reduce the number of plaits which will make the front look more compact.

It becomes more complicated when you also want to change, visually, the shape of the topline of the neck, by doing high plaits and tight plaits or a combination of both. High plaits have more body, since they are built from a longer, thicker mane, and are basically stitched within the hair of the plait which rests above the topline rather than on the side of the neck, which is normal. This gives a pony more depth of crest and is ideal for those animals that are immature. Tight plaits are the opposite; often quite small, they are stitched below the topline in the hope of lowering the arch of the crest – the best results ensue from short, well-pulled manes.

If a pony is plain in the head, make the first plait a high one as this will help to make the head look as though it fits neatly onto the neck. If a pony's muscle dips away in front of the wither (often seen in older animals) the gap can be filled better with a few high plaits, thereby taking the rainbow effect from the point of the wither to the poll. Using a combination of all types of plait to create a really good front requires much practice, and the change from one type to another must be done well and gradually so as not to lose the continuity of outline.

High plaits: (above) Start to plait in an upward motion about 1½in from the roots; (right) Take the needle through and under the plait, about 2in from the roots; (bottom left) Wrap the cotton around the plait, working downwards, and stitch through the fold at the bottom – the plait is now half the length but double the thickness; (right) Roll the plait into the cobra-like hood, and secure the plaited ball. (Main picture) It can be seen how plaits have given the neck more height

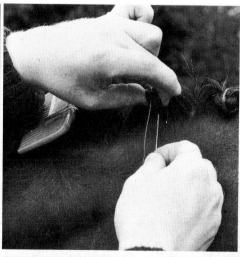

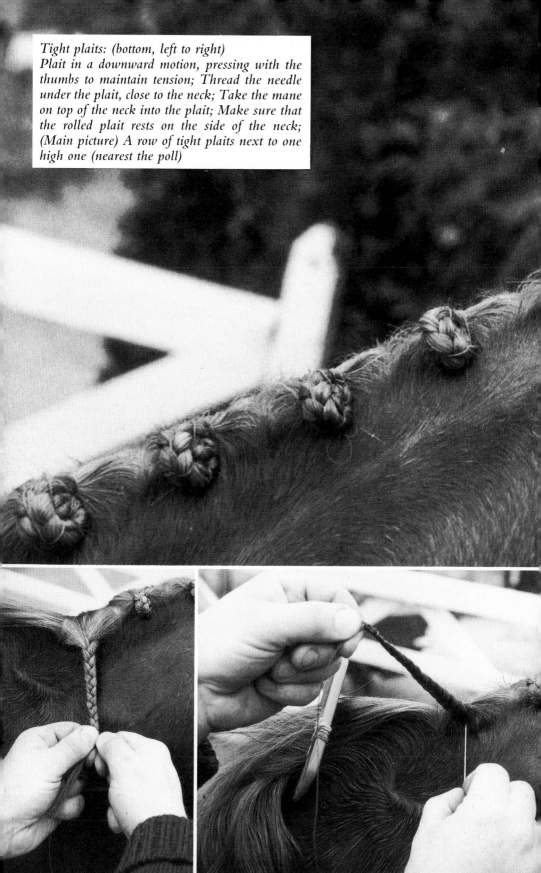

Tight plaits: (bottom, left to right)
Plait in a downward motion, pressing with the
thumbs to maintain tension; Thread the needle
under the plait, close to the neck; Take the mane
on top of the neck into the plait; Make sure that
the rolled plait rests on the side of the neck;
(Main picture) A row of tight plaits next to one
high one (nearest the poll)

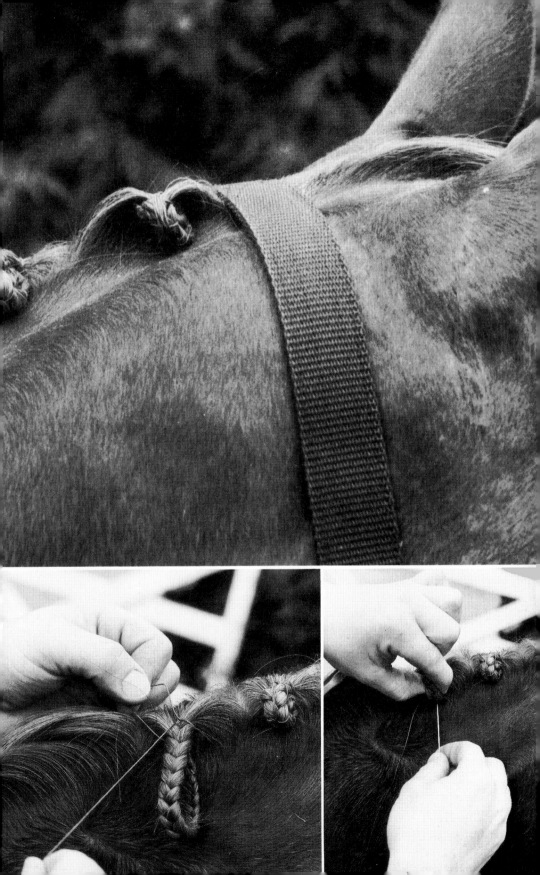

High Plaits

When doing high plaits, the plaiter may have to stand on a milk crate so as to work above the pony. Take up three sections of mane as normal and start to plait about 1½in (37mm) from the roots in an upward motion. The plait itself should be tight, and use the thumbs to keep the portions of hair locked into each other all the time – people often think that because the high plait is a loose type, the plaiting itself should be slack, which is not the case. Secure the end of each plait as normal and sew with the needle through and under the plait about 2in (50mm) from the roots. Wrap the cotton around the plait working downwards and stitch through the fold at the bottom. The length of the plait is half the size but double the thickness at this stage. Then roll the plait into the cobra-like hood you have created at the roots and secure this plaited ball (which at this stage can be moulded into the right place with the fingers) by threading the needle through the plait a few times, making sure that the thread does not slip to either side thereby damaging the hood effect. From both off- and near-side, it will be quite clear that the plaits give the neck more height.

Tight Plaits

When doing tight plaits, start at the roots and plait in a downward manner; pull with each plaiting movement and press on the hair with the thumbs to maintain the tension, as the length of plait must not buckle when being rolled up. Secure the ends as normal and thread the needle under the plait as close to the neck as possible, threading through one side of the plait and then the other so that the mane on top of the neck is included in the plait and does not have the hood effect as with the high plait. Continue as before, only make sure that when the plait is rolled into a ball it rests on the side of the neck instead of on top or above the topline. Secure the plait by stitching – again, loop the cotton either side of the plait for extra security, and flatten any hood effect that may occur.

If there are any sprutty bits of mane after plaiting is finished, it is quite possible to break all the rules and get rid of these either by tweaking them out or cutting them off. Some people may be horrified by this suggestion, yet why not have everything looking right for that particular day? – why spoil the picture as you wait for half a season for loose hair to grow enough to be included in the plaits? After all, the pony may go lame at any time, in which case it won't need plaiting at all!

If the mane in front of the wither area is too short to plait, rather than leave it which looks untidy, try and sew it into small nodules which look like plaits – often this means stitching into a lot of cotton rather than a lot of hair! Hair as short as this *can* sometimes be plaited if wax or resin is used to make it more manageable.

Unplaiting

Untold damage can be done if unplaiting is done in a rush and special care must be taken not to snip hair near the roots by mistake, resulting in clumps of mane falling to the floor. If an animal is to be re-plaited soon afterwards, always water-brush the mane so that the hair goes back to normal; it is very difficult to make a neat job of replaiting the heavy tresses which remain after unplaiting.

PLAITING A TAIL

I like to see a well pulled tail in the show ring in preference to a plaited one. However, the latter can certainly look the part if done correctly, especially in in-hand classes. Unfortunately, many people plait it too tightly in an effort to do a neat job, and to try and make sure the plait stops in position during the show, and as a result foals and youngsters can be seen going short behind and clamping their tails down, which judges do not like to see. The plaited tail should keep its shape if sprayed with hair spray or dabbed with setting gel prior to tail bandaging. But remember to unravel the bandage when taking it off, rather than pulling it off as is normal with a pulled tail.

Make sure that the tail is clean and well brushed before attempting to plait – the job is difficult enough without making it harder still. Some people prefer to plait with a dry tail, others work better when it has been wetted with a water brush. The secret is not to take too much hair at once, otherwise the plait will become too thick to work with and will appear untidy; also, make sure that the hair you use is in sections of equal size. Take a section of hair from either side and cross the right-hand section over the left; then introduce a third piece from the left and a fourth piece from the right, and so on, so that you are working down the tail adding from alternate sides. Some people take the third piece from the centre to start with, and then take from alternate sides after that. Whichever method you choose, keep your plait firm and use your thumbs to keep the tension as you do when

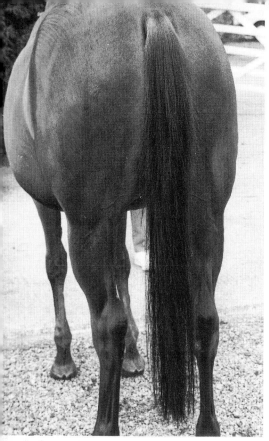

1 The tail must be clean and well brushed before plaiting is attempted

2 Take a section of hair from either side, and cross right over left; then introduce a third section from the left

3 Work down the tail

4 Keep the plait firm: use the thumbs to maintain tension

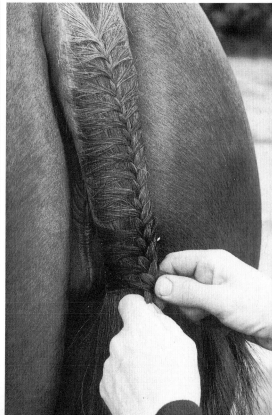

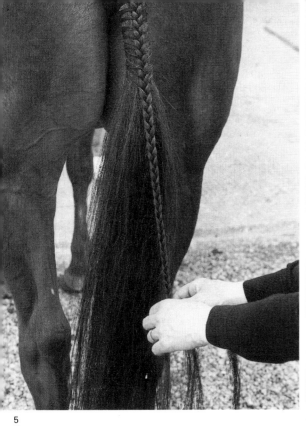

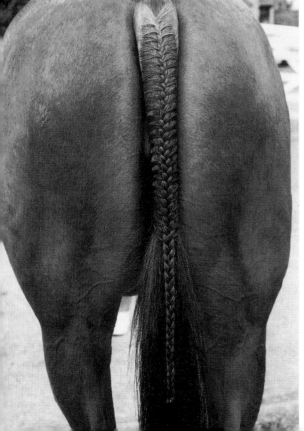

5
9

6

7

8

5 Once the end of the dock has been reached, make a normal plait until the ends of the hair sections are reached

6 Secure the plait with cotton

7 Double the long plait under, and secure in position

8 Stitch up and down the length of a double plait to make it lie flat

9 The finished product

plaiting a mane. Depending on personal preference and what suits the animal best, continue plaiting until you reach somewhere around the end of the dock; then continue making a normal plait for the full length of the three pieces. Secure the end with cotton and then double this long plait under; stitch up and down along this double plait to make it lie flat, and secure with a knot. You can easily become an expert with practice. Perhaps the hardest tails to plait are those of foals (which have very baby, bushy hair) which wriggle about at important moments during plaiting.

THE FINISHING TOUCHES

When getting your show animal ready for the ring, we will assume that he has already had a good groom, particularly around the head, and that his feet have been picked out beforehand. There are several things that can now be applied to give the picture that expert finish, just as car enthusiasts wax their vehicle after washing.

Gloss and Polish

We put show-gloss spray on our animals (keeping it away from the head region), unless it is absolutely pouring down with rain when it would be a waste of time. This helps to give a better depth of shine which will last for a few days, and is particularly useful if the animal is showing on consecutive days; it also helps to keep its coat dust-free. By adjusting the nozzle, the show sheen can be sprayed on very finely which will avoid a blotchy finish, and then wiped evenly into the coat with a clean stable rubber. This type of spray application is very useful when using fly repellent, and far better than wiping the animal down with a cloth dampened with fly-spray liquid, which more often than not leaves wet streaks on the pony's coat.

The head and legs can be polished using 'Vitalis' hair dressing, rubbed down on a cloth – a useful tip if your animal looks common-limbed. Brilliantine can be used to add a glistening touch to tails and plaits, though not always on greys as they can look grubby with certain types of oily coat dressing; remember also that clear setting gel has already been used on the tail prior to tail bandaging, and on the plaits to help keep their shape. Be careful with coloured setting gel, especially on grey tails.

If a pony has a particularly high tail carriage, some people wet the bottom of the tail to try and weigh it down a little – and believe it or not, this does sometimes work!

Highlighting the Head

Black stage makeup (which can be bought in crayon form) blended with liquid paraffin or baby oil and used discreetly around the eyes and muzzle, can give a sharper outline just as blusher can to a lady's face, and can sometimes make even a piggy eye look more generous. However, be careful not to use it too heavily – some show ponies have been brought into the ring looking like giant pandas! It can also be used to highlight black joints on legs or to camouflage hairs which following injury have re-grown white, although black printers' ink in tube form is also ideal for this purpose.

Some people still use vaseline on the eyes and muzzle, although this does attract dust because it is in jelly form. Printers' ink and baby oil can also be used to improve the jawline of grey ponies whose heads are generally a lighter colour than the rest of the body, making them look as though they were set on to the neck as an afterthought. With this sort of camouflaging it is important not to alter the identification marks of an animal; and also applies when highlighting (rather than enlarging) a white star on a pony's forehead. One respected judge once sent a pony which was standing top out of the ring at a qualifying show, because a white star had been quite blatantly painted on the pony's forehead.

White Socks

After the shoe-whitener or ceiling white has been brushed out of white socks, loose chalk powder or talcum powder is the best for getting them really white and bright. Chalk blocks can sometimes leave streaks, especially with particularly fluted tendon areas.

Hoof Oil

A special black hoof-oil cream can be used on the hooves; our farrier was particularly pleased with this, as opposed to the nail-varnish type black hoof polish which stayed on the hooves like concrete. Liquid black shoe polish can also be used on the hooves, finished off with a clear hoof oil to make them shine. Four black hooves always presents a more balanced picture, even though this sometimes means blacking out a white foot – an odd-coloured foot, just as an odd white sock, can sometimes make a pony look lame in the judge's eyes.

With a 'hard' colour the coat should be healthy and shining; when getting a grey ready for the ring, the object is to have this colour dazzling rather than merely shining – just as you can see in the soap powder advertisements on the television!

117

Quarter Marks

One of the final finishing touches before going into the ring is the application of quarter marks to the hindquarters; these are achieved by combing or brushing the coat in different directions with a comb or stiff body brush. They need not be just for decoration; used cleverly they can usually improve the shape of the hindquarters, whether it be a conformation fault, weakness or simply lack of condition. Some people do put them in merely for decoration, or because it seems to be the 'in' thing to do, and can in their ignorance exaggerate a weakness, especially if the squares and patterns are uneven or incomplete. The outcome is usually, however, very good, both for those who can draw the squares on very quickly as much as for others who seem to take for ever, making sure that every square is a perfect copy of the others.

As well as a fairly new body brush, it is advisable to have a varied selection of combs (of different widths), as obviously a bigger horse will require patterns of a larger size, whereas a lead-rein pony will look better with smaller ones. Some people use a small section of comb, whilst others take all the teeth out of a long comb except for the first few and then use the frame of the comb as a handle. This also helps them to judge a straight line. To give squares and sharks' teeth patterns more definition, it is advisable to use a water brush to wet the hair beforehand, or possibly setting gel – they will then be more permanent and will need only touching up later in the day. The use of hair spray to keep them in shape is also highly favoured.

When practising at home, look at the quarters objectively and think which type of marking will suit the pony best; do the quarters slope away badly or are they very flat? do they lack scope? and are they weak looking? Some quarters look better for being filled and others look better with more simple markings, which are less busy and are not drawing attention to a particular fault. In any case, some quarters are just not big enough for teeth, squares and lines. When competing in hunter-type classes, less fancy, more workmanlike block-type squares are better, especially with big horses.

The golden rule is that the starting line for the squares must always be parallel to the ground line and must not follow the contour of the quarters; this is one reason why the commercial plastic stencils do not always work, because they follow the line of the quarters – this would particularly defeat the object if the quarters themselves sloped away badly. To cover this particular fault, make the squares slightly deeper on the tail side in an attempt to build up the offending slope, and start high enough up the quarter to fill it as much as possible. Quarters which lack scope can also be improved by drawing longer squares and by using the full width and depth of the quarter area – be sure to start high enough, and work down to a point a little lower down than normal.

When using a triangle shape, some quarters look better when the shape is wider and shorter as opposed to being narrower and longer. Sharks' teeth can be used to fill a hollower side and make a weak second thigh look stronger. Brush marks need to be done cleverly otherwise they can break up a quarter badly, but in general they do help to make the quarters look stronger and symmetrical, especially when standing behind the animal. If the quarters are very flat and square-looking, use good sweeping curves with sharks' teeth and bigger brush marks, and the picture will look a lot more pleasing to the eye.

If the quarters slope away, be very careful with the brush marks – in some cases it may be better to dispense with these altogether. We have experimented with other patterns in place of squares in the past, especially in the pairs classes when the turnout and colour schemes can be a little more fun and outrageous. A particular success was a shamrock which looked very different and very effective in its simplicity!

There are no hard and fast rules when applying the finishing touches; you must use your eye quite a lot, and be prepared to experiment in order to achieve that breathtaking picture.

CHAPTER 7

Tack and Turnout

TACK

No matter what type of tack you use, make sure that it is of good quality, clean and well maintained, and that it enhances the appearance of your show animal. For instance, cheap, bright orange saddles with staples and studs are unsightly and economically a waste of money. Saddles with holes in them, with the padding exposed and broken trees, bridles with chewed reins and rusty buckles, and stirrup leathers with rotten stitching reflect badly on your production, like all dirty tack, quite apart from being counter-productive and downright dangerous; and sadly this is seen far too often in the show rings.

One young enthusiast once sought out the stables of a horse that had just been made champion hack at a very big show, on the chance of seeing and admiring the production at close quarters – only to be amazed at seeing a saddle being removed from the horse which was so thick with grease that it could not have been cleaned for weeks. He never looked on that professional yard in the same light from that moment on.

Clever use of tack can visually alter the true picture and cover up faults like a plain head or a long back, although in the case of the latter the illusion is short-lived if the pony is stripped during a class. Tack will also, of course, determine the way the horse goes and the comfort of the ride. Brand-new tack takes a long time to break in, especially saddles – we buy it only when absolutely necessary – but luckily there is a good second-hand market, since owners seem to change animals and consequently tack on a regular basis; most saddlers have a good range of second-hand quality tack for sale. New tack must never be worn in the ring without being darkened with neatsfoot oil or the equivalent; for best results, warm the oil in an old saucepan on the stove first which will make the oil more fluid – it will then soak into the tack more quickly as well as darkening it faster. However, be careful, as leather will go very spongey and slippery if over-oiled, quite apart from leaving stains on clothing and your lovely grey horse! One of the biggest headaches is when part of a bridle needs to be replaced and has to be darkened to match the rest of the bridle.

Those bridles which are obviously made up of bits and pieces, with odd cheek pieces and so on, can spoil the overall picture and will simply not do. Because delicate show tack is so expensive, a separate set of more workmanlike tack is essential. The only time our show tack is used on an every-day basis is when it is being broken in or when we are trying it out for appearance and comfort.

Saddles

There are many different types of saddle to choose from these days, but above all a saddle must fit the animal in question well, and must give a comfortable ride. Some of today's equine physiotherapists believe that saddles should have a larger bearing surface, thus spreading the rider's weight more evenly; also that a smoother stuffing be used to avoid the rocking effect some older saddles produce when panels become firm and rounded – and maintain that both would go a long way towards eliminating back problems in horses.

A judge of ridden horses may have to sit on a range of different saddles in one class; some of them slip forwards and others may be like sitting on a wooden board, and this can sometimes influence his decision on an animal's ride. Some of the show saddles with the straight-cut flaps – the idea being to reveal a good shoulder – are more often than not monsters to ride in, which is why you see so many children slipping about in the saddle and unable to ride their ponies properly. If a small jockey is insecure in the saddle, some of the dressage-type show saddles are ideal as the knee roll is a fairly straight cut yet gives the jockey that extra bit of strength in the leg.

Another common sight is to see jockeys riding in saddles which are either too small or too big for them, so they are either sprawling over the sides or getting left behind the movement in a vast, soup-plate seat. Luckily in pony classes, there are only two points to consider when choosing a saddle: that it fits the rider and the pony. However, in ridden horse classes, the judge must also be accommodated, and he will probably be a lot bigger than the jockey. This point is particularly relevant when a large male judge is expected to sit on a hack belonging to a small lady who rides in a very deep, short-coupled dressage saddle; in some cases he may refuse to ride the animal if he thinks the saddle is unsuitable and would cause extreme discomfort.

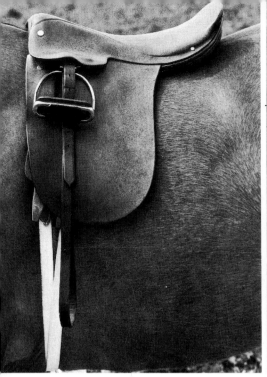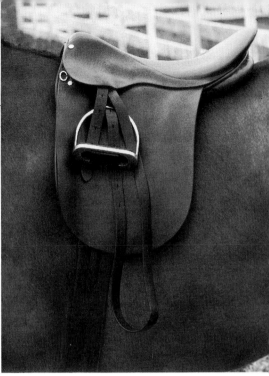

(Left) A show saddle with a narrow white show girth. Note that the underneath strap is at the front

(Right) A dressage-type show saddle with a dark Cottage Craft girth

Judges generally like the Owen-type saddles, especially hunter judges, because they feel closer to the horse, rather than perched miles above the animal like the princess and the pea! Some of the well used dressage-type saddles, however, can be equally suitable for lady judges. Avoid those with high cantles that tip the rider forward – and, of course, those that squeak! Most show saddles in the ring are fairly straight cut, although the general purpose type is ideal for working hunter classes because it allows the jockey to adopt a jumping position which is necessary if he is to ride the large tracks sometimes seen at the bigger shows. Show jumping saddles tend to cover up too much of the shoulder to be any good for showing purposes.

At the end of the day you must also take the trouble to choose a saddle which looks good on your horse – sometimes a smaller saddle will give a very short-coupled animal a bit more scope, just as a big saddle can also be used to cover up a long back. Saddle flaps are also quite important – if they are too small they can make an animal appear pot-bellied or too deep. Saddles with a cut-back head are suitable for an animal with a very high wither;

and a saddle with a raised cantle will help to camouflage a dipped back.

Some saddles are too heavy which can lead to all sorts of problems; this is often true of side saddles, which must fit a horse securely and be level – if there is too little stuffing then the rider will be thrown to the back of the saddle and if the stuffing is uneven, she will be thrown to one side or the other. A horse's saddle region can be hardened by dabbing on surgical spirit, particularly before using a side saddle. One important point to remember when putting on a side saddle is to fasten the girth straps *gradually*, especially the balance straps so that the horse doesn't have a bucking fit. It may even be necessary to give your horse a quick lunge before getting on board.

Bridles
In the bridle department, one of the most common mistakes that people make is to use a very fine bridle simply because it is a show class, and this often makes their animal look plain in the head. A small pony with a dainty head will look attractive in a fine bridle, but progressively up through the heights the leather work needs to be more sensible, and must fit the job in question. For instance, a heavyweight hunter will look better in a plain wide browband and noseband rather than a fancy stitched one which is more suitable for hacks – it is surprising how many people use very fine, coloured browbands even on bigger horses when a wider one would suit better.

It is also important to note that in hunter type classes, coloured browbands are taboo in the show ring just as they would be in the hunting field. If a horse is plain in the head, in the case of a hunter just use wider leather to cover it up; for a hack or a show pony, you can use wider leather and a flashy wider browband. Remember that with coloured browbands, the darker colour should always be on top.

Not every show animal has a perfect head, and it is the producer's job to conceal it as well as possible. I remember taking a new client down to Andy Crofts' to look at a young 14.2hh pony; it was a strong sort although a little plain in the head, but nevertheless a good pony (as results proved later on) and particularly correct in its conformation. They turned the animal down because they didn't like its head, despite being advised that this was a minor problem which could be overcome with correct bridling – much better this than to have a bad hindleg, which even the best man in the country would have a job to cover up.

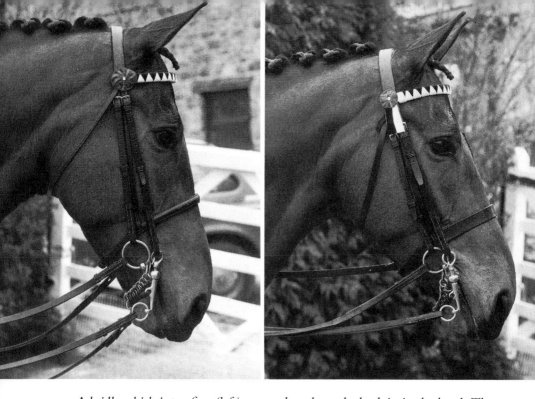

A bridle which is too fine (left) can make a horse look plain in the head. The chunkier bridle on the right is more sensible – apart from the chewed rein! (Opposite) A pelham bridle (left) can sometimes leave a head looking very bare. Adding a second cheekpiece can solve the problem

Bridles for the Individual

Bridles are often bought complete, but sometimes these do need adjusting to suit individual requirements. This rule applies to nearly every area of production – each animal is an individual, just as humans are all different. For instance, an animal may need a wider noseband either to break up a white blaze or if it is very straight of its head; some need a wider throat-latch, particularly if they have too strong a jawline – and if an animal has a somewhat Arab look to its jaw, having a slightly looser throat-latch will make this look less obvious than if it is fitted tightly.

Ponies can look plain in the head when wearing a snaffle bridle or a pelham bridle because of the single cheek pieces which leave the head more exposed; with a snaffle use thicker leather, and with a pelham use a second (bridoon) cheek-piece for cosmetic purposes only, attaching it to the top rein like you would with a Rugby pelham.

If an animal is produced and going correctly you will not notice a plain head so much, and if it does have one it is not the end of

the world, as the show animal does not, after all, operate with its head – in many ways it is better to have a good set of limbs and feet.

Make sure that all strap ends and loose pieces of leather are securely tucked into their respective keepers – flapping cheek pieces can look very untidy, and so, particularly, can the noseband.

Reins

Reins need to be light and supple in the hand but not flimsy; they are the connecting cable to the horse's mouth. For a jockey who has bad hands, stiffer thicker reins can be used, as they are more difficult to grab hold of than thinner reins which are more sensitive on the mouth in this situation. They want to be neither too long nor too short, or you will either be constantly riding on the buckle end, or will have great loops of leather dangling at your feet – which can also, of course, be dangerous. I prefer to have a slightly thicker top rein (bridoon rein), and when jumping or in a hunter-type class where the animal is going to take you on a bit more, a plaited rein will give you more grip – those which are half plaited are very smart. Rubber reins or continental canvas reins are accepted in working classes but are really more suitable for the hunting field; coloured reins, however, in both hunting field and show ring are not acceptable. Reins with buckles at the end are preferable to the stitched sort, just in case a horse doesn't like reins going over his head, in which case the buckled variety can be undone.

These days, the double reins which join together so that they form one in the rider's hand are not seen very much, but are ideal for smaller jockeys who have trouble holding two reins. To overcome this problem, some of these used to ride in a single rein pelham such as a globe pelham; this did not always produce the desired result, however, as the action of riding on a single curb with inexperienced hands made the pony very overbent.

Bits

Although stitched bridles are very neat they do not give much scope if you like to change bits regularly. Without going into too much detail regarding bits, as it is up to the individual to decide which bit suits a particular animal (which is in itself an art), there are some common-sense ground rules which can be discussed. Someone once said that 'there are no bad mouths in horses, just bad hands on riders'; and thus the other expression, 'it takes two to pull'. Some bits suit some animals better than others and experimenting at the beginning of a season is not a bad idea, although if an animal is wrong with his teeth and sore in the mouth there will always be problems no matter what bit you choose. This is one reason that we have the horse dentist on a regular basis; if he has given each horse the OK, and a problem does occur, we then know that it could be a resistance rather than a wolf tooth rearing its ugly head.

The general rule is that the thicker and simpler the bit the kinder it is on the mouth, and the thinner and more fancy it is, the more severe the action will be on the bars of the mouth. For example, the straight-bar or half-moon snaffle is a lot milder than the jointed type of bit which creates a nutcracker action causing more pressure; and the rougher the texture — whether it be a simple twisted snaffle or one with rollers — the more pressure again, since it will prevent the pony from leaning on the bit. Without putting anyone at risk, the less capable the jockey is, the more simple the bit should be, so that there is less damage done to the animal's mouth.

Whatever bit you choose, make sure that it is not too narrow, when it will pinch the sides of the mouth; nor too wide, which can look very unsightly. It must also be high enough in the mouth; having it too low is often the reason for the horse getting his tongue over the bit — tightening the noseband and using a tongue-guard or grid will also be useful if this particular problem continues. Without going over the top, having bits higher in the mouth can also make some animals more 'set up' in their bridle, just as the thin, overcheck bridoon bits can work in the same way.

Double bridles are more commonly favoured in the ring because they can work in two different ways – riders should be able to use both reins independently of each other to achieve maximum benefit. For instance, riding on the top rein is like riding in a snaffle and can be used to pick a horse up into its bridle; whereas the curb rein can be used to make a horse flex more, and works as the brake. If a horse has been introduced from a snaffle to a double bridle correctly there is no reason why he shouldn't accept it. However, sometimes it is necessary to use the pelham, particularly with a young animal, as a stepping stone.

The action of a pelham is basically a lot kinder and simpler than a double bridle, and is particularly effective if an animal has a high head carriage and needs to be persuaded to work a lot lower – although after a while it may learn to lean badly on a pelham. It is basically a snaffle with a curb; if an animal is not ready for a double bit but would look more dressed up with double reins – which would particularly apply in an open class – the pelham would be ideal.

I have always preferred a jointed bit to a straight-bar one, even shortly after breaking, because it gives more control and a better feeling of direction. A key bit after a while can teach a horse to play with his tongue.

Bitting

There are so many variations amongst all the bits being used today; basically it depends what you want a bit to do. For instance, the long, fixed cheek-piece in a Weymouth or pelham will give you more leverage and braking power than a short moveable one. Bits can be made milder if bandaged with gamgee or elasticated tape, or leather which has been washed; if these are then soaked in treacle or suchlike it will make the horse salivate more. Bits made from different materials will have different results, whether they are made from vulcanite, copper or even soft rubber; the latter is suitable for youngsters or those with sensitive mouths. Stainless steel is preferable to nickel.

Some animals will go better if they have a strange bit in their mouths all of a sudden, which is why riding in a double bridle all the time, during the summer, is not a good thing – much better to work at home in a snaffle and ride in the double on the day before a show, thereby letting the double bits have maximum 'surprise' effect.

Some owners need to ride their horses in a different bit every week to keep it interested and bridling. I remember being in Ruth McMullen's caravan on Herts County showground a few years ago, and she had a pillowcase full of bits; she had already used several only that morning whilst working in a difficult light-weight hunter, before she was happy with the way he was going – the idea being that a new bit in his mouth would make him think about his job until such time as its magic wore off!

An effective schooling snaffle is the four ring one; this puts a good mouth on a horse and can be used either with the snaffle bit moving through the rings held by the cheek-pieces, or more fixed with the reins on the inner rings and the snaffle rings held by the cheek pieces. A butterfly bit will stop some ponies rolling their tongues over the bit, and rather than a dropped noseband in this particular case, try doing up the cavesson noseband tight to stop a pony from opening its mouth. Pelhams with high ports (rather than the half-moon types), Rugby pelhams and fixed-sided Weymouths have all been used by us with great success.

The butterfly bit

It is the producer's job to make sure that the animal is bridled well, but be careful – it may offend the judge if he looks into the pony's mouth and finds some sort of mediaeval contraption!

Curb Chains

There are many types of curb chain to use, and remember that it is correct for these to be accompanied by a leather lip-strap; always check that they are not twisted. Of the metal ones, the close-linked ones are better than the more open-ringed ones, and are the strongest type to use. Make sure that the hooks are not too big and are sufficiently open to allow the chain to be hooked on so that it will neither come loose nor take half-an-hour to get off. If you are shortening or tightening a curb chain by hooking more rings, keep these even to both sides as it looks smarter.

As an alternative to metal curb chains, there are the less severe, elastic ones and also leather ones. If the curb chain is only on for show, it is far better to use a loose elastic or leather one because a loose metal one will jangle and is untidy, and may even annoy the pony – in this case it may be better to remove it altogether. A point to remember is that some elasticated curb chains do shrink when washed, so be careful. An amusing sight concerning curb chains and often seen in the rings, is of a rider further down the line undoing the curb chain, having watched a ham-fisted judge ride the first two horses badly, in the hope of giving his horse an easier time!

Numnahs

There are many types of numnah on the market which are basically used to protect the horse's back. In the show ring these are ideal if an animal is cold-backed, but they are also useful for cosmetic purposes, especially if an animal is dipped or long in the back, or needs to feel softer in the ride. Some people use them if their mount has a sore back, but if this is the case one should really consider whether the horse should be ridden at all.

The worst type are the chunky sheepskin ones, which drown the horse and really belong as a rug at the bedside; they also make the saddle slip and the judge feel as though he is two feet off the horse's back. Whether a full numnah is used or a sheepskin pad, it must be securely fitted to the shape of the saddle and not be allowed to slip which can make a horse's back sore. This can also look very unsightly in the ring, as though you had a pet animal hiding under the saddle which has come up for air! Always make sure that the front of the numnah is pulled up so that it is not tight over the withers or the spine, and above all make sure that it is clean. Dried sweat can rub against the horse's coat and scald the back.

The darker-coloured numnahs (black and brown – never use red or blue ones) are more commonly used these days and blend well with the rest of the horse's tack. However, if an animal is a dark colour, a light numnah with a white girth can sometimes look very sharp and very much the part in a hack class. White

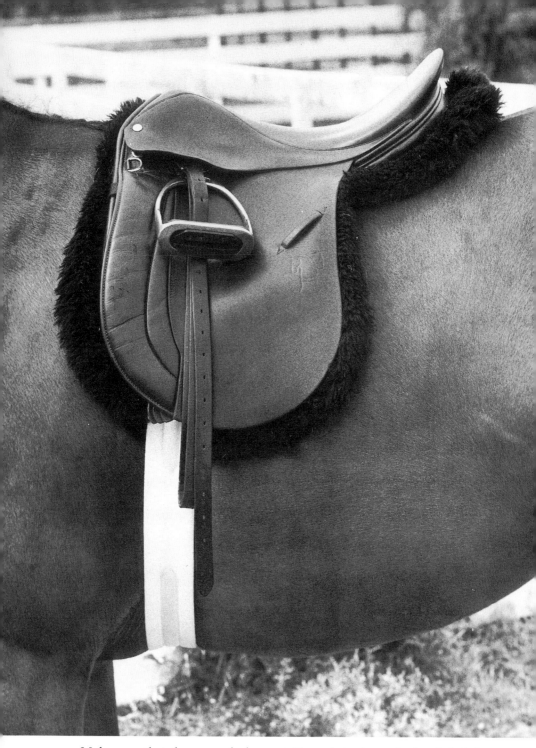

Make sure that the nummah does not 'drown' the horse (unless it is being used to cover up a long or dipped back), and that a white girth does not visually cut an animal in two

girths do tend to cut an animal in two visually (unless used on greys); this is perfectly all right if that particular horse has good balanced conformation, but if this is not the case it can exaggerate the fact that it may have a good front but a very weak hind leg, which would be less noticeable at first glance if the girth blended with the colour of the horse.

Girths

We use the Cottage Craft type girths which come in brown, black and white; they are easily washable, they are wide enough to keep a saddle in place, and are soft on an animal's skin – it is also easy to tighten this kind of girth without feeling that you are cutting the horse in two. For this reason the narrow, white canvas-type girths with the rubber centre are not so good, but if they are used, remember to have the under-strap as the forward girth to avoid trapping the pony's skin.

In horse classes and hunter-type classes leather girths are excellent, and are hardwearing providing they are kept supple. We have a couple of three-fold girths in the tack-room which have given us good service over the years; mostly we use balding girths which allow the air to circulate. These girths are narrow in the centre and reduce the chance of rubbing. When tightening any girth which has a middle plate, keep this plate in the middle – not, as is sometimes seen, with the middle plate halfway up one side because the girth has been fastened up more on one side than the other.

Buckle guards are a good idea to protect the underside of the saddle flaps and to prevent the buckles hurting the rider's knees. However, have the girth straps of a dressage saddle altered so that they will take an ordinary girth; those that fasten at stirrup level are not suitable for the show ring.

Stirrup Irons

Stainless steel stirrup irons are best and do not need as much polishing as nickel ones. They must be well fitting, ideally with ½in (12mm) free on either side between the iron and the foot, although they must be big enough – like stirrup leathers – to accommodate a variety of sizes of judge. Safety stirrups are ideal for children, with the rubber band worn on the outside. Rubber treads in the stirrup are a must to help prevent the rider's foot from slipping – far too many riders can be seen with the toe, rather than the ball of the foot, resting in the stirrups which often results in a leg position which is too far forward.

Martingales

Some yards use various types of tack more than others; for instance, we are not fans of dropped nosebands, but always like to exercise in running martingales at home. A standing martingale simply prevents the horse from throwing its head in the air, whereas the running martingale helps to maintain a good headcarriage more directly from the bit. A running martingale is very often fitted too slack so that it has no effect whatsoever, or so short that it has a severe lever action on the mouth: correctly fitted, the rings should be in line with the animal's withers. Leather or dark rubber stoppers should be used on the reins to prevent the rings from getting stuck on the bit buckles of the reins, and the neck-strap should be neither too loose nor too tight, and with the ends secured by a keeper.

Both types of martingale are accepted in the working hunter type classes, especially with a snaffle bridle; however, some judges may deduct a mark or two if the running martingale is attached to the curb rein on a double bridle. The smaller children sometimes find the neck-strap useful when jumping over some of the bigger fences.

The Overall Effect

Tack must therefore be practical and comfortable; and tack chosen carefully can also help to create a certain picture. For example, one year we had a horse which finished reserve champion hack at White City, and the next day competed in the riding horse class where he came second. Even though it wasn't the same judge, we tried to alter the picture so that people wouldn't even think it was the same horse. In the hacks, he had a bridle with brass clips and sported a very smart coloured browband, a white girth and a suede show saddle; in the riding horses he had a bigger, stronger bridle with a plain browband, and a more general purpose saddle with a leather girth, besides which his rider wore a plain tweed jacket. And it worked – a lot of people thought we had been showing two different horses!

The canter should be smooth and elegant. Royal Return, many times Champion Hack, including Wembley in 1980, and described by the late Count Robert Orssich as 'a rarity – a true hack!'

The correct dress for hack finals: Robert Oliver on Tomadachi (which means 'my friend' in Japanese), and Carol Gilbert-Scott (behind) on Chancley Voodoo

The 14.2hh show pony Runnings Park Hill Star, produced by the author and Champion at Wembley, the Royal International Horse Show and the Royal Show

TURNOUT

Street fashion may change, but riding wear in the show ring remains consistently conservative, which after all is not a bad thing as it is the horse which should attract the judge's eye. Robert Oliver maintains that 'the best dressed person is the one whose clothes attract the least attention'. Outfits which diverge from this opinion are sometimes seen in the show pony classes, especially with handlers in the lead rein class. A few years ago, the in-hand classes saw a young lady doing her own thing when Sarah Watchorn showed Cusop Delightful to become supreme champion at the Royal wearing a mini-skirt!

It is amazing how people will turn themselves out badly and spoil the overall picture, having spent a fortune on feed and a vast amount of time on producing their animals to look so well. Ronnie Marmont is the doyen of turnout, and says, 'Showing is like being on the stage and you have to look your best especially on the big occasion.' Many a bad rider can look more competent by looking smart and the main objective is to look professional, rather than appearing like a plastic Moss Bros dummy in your brand-new outfit, or too serviceable like an old hand in an outfit that has seen out two wars and been passed on down through the family!

Good quality clothing will last longer – you pay for what you get these days, and although it may be a little more expensive initially, it will stand the hard wear that riding in all weathers and being with animals demands. Because of this there is quite a strong second-hand clothing market in operation which must not be dismissed, as often these garments are made of better quality materials than the present-day, brand-new items.

Hats
No matter in which class you are showing, you must have a hat that fits well – even in the yard, when working on the ground, a hard hat should in some situations be worn for safety; and a well fitting hat means there is no need for elastic under the chin (except, of course, for skull caps). However, some very young children do need to wear elastic just in case, as it is extremely difficult to get a hat to fit in this age range. Pink knicker elastic is no longer acceptable; it was seen quite frequently a few years ago and looked very ghoulish, the idea being that the colour would blend with the skin – some parents must have had very funny coloured children!

135

Locks and Herbert Johnson are still the best hatters around and offer many different shapes and styles to suit every stature and face. Some ladies can look quite fearsome when wearing an over-large bowler hat! And it is surprising how many parents buy their tall children the high-crowned riding hats which make them look even bigger on their ponies. There are some comical sights to be seen in the adult classes, too – especially those bowlers that are flat and wide in the brim and look as though they need pipes and guttering, often perched on the back of the head.

It is also amazing how many people buy the wrong top hat, possibly thinking that they will only wear it twice a year, so it won't really matter. However, consider this – if you *are* lucky enough to do well in the finals at the RIHS or Wembley, it seems such a shame that the photograph taken for posterity of your very shiny, classy animal is going to be marred by you, because you are doing a good imitation of the Mad Hatter or look as if you've been hit over the head with a sledgehammer!

I was very lucky with my top hat – it cost £25 from a friend, and I discovered later that it belonged to a Victorian dance troup and was worth four times as much!

No matter what hat you get, it must be worn straight on the head, it must fit well – you never know when you might fall off – and be comfortable. Think how many hours it will be worn in a busy show season – you will hardly be able to concentrate on the job in hand when in the ring if your ill-fitting hat is giving you a blinding headache.

Hats can be cleaned by brushing, then wipe the dust away with a damp cloth and wet steam very lightly over a kettle. Another point is that to be strictly correct the ribbon at the back of a cap should be sewn up.

Hair

The hair style should complement whichever type of hat is worn, but it would take too long to discuss this point, and at the end of the day it is a matter of personal choice anyway – except for those gentlemen like myself who seem to be losing their hair at a fast rate these days, which significantly reduces the options open! However, one point which *is* worth mentioning, is that hair needs to be tidy; this means that gentlemen should have it cut short and not look like something from 'Top of the Pops', and ladies should have it secured, either in a net or in plaits or suchlike, and should not look like a model in a shampoo advert!

We see a variety of styles in pony classes, from bunches to hair which has been flicked back and set – these poor children have often had to spend the previous night in agony with rollers and grips, looking like junior versions of Ena Sharples in order to perfect the hair style for the big day. These are all interesting and on the whole look very good, providing, of course, that mothers do not go over the top with the hair ribbons and make the child look gift-wrapped!

Young female jockeys seem to be growing up much more quickly these days and use make-up a lot more – this is acceptable in the older jockeys, providing it is done in moderation. I have heard two 14.2hh jockeys talking about flashing themselves up because a Mr . . . is judging their class later in the day – this is pushing the concern for getting noticed a bit too far!

Jackets

About fifteen years ago there was a fashion in pony classes to show in jackets of various colours – green, grey, maroon and so on; in fact there was a family who lived nearby who were known as the 'plum Jacksons' for this reason. This may add to the variety, but really nothing can beat either a navy show jacket – black can look too sombre with children and ladies, especially on a nervous jockey who will look as white as a sheet – or a nice tweed coat; this should not be too flashy or else you will look like a bookie's runner, and it can have one or two vents, whichever suits your shape.

No-one can beat Bernard Weatherill jackets, and although they are expensive, think how many times a jacket will be worn during a show season. A teenager who needs a tweed jacket should buy the best that he or she can afford – persuade mother and father to send you to Weatherills at Christmas time or on your birthday and treat you to a jacket as an investment. I had ten years' wear out of mine until I outgrew it, and then we sold it for a reasonable sum simply because the make was good.

It does, admittedly, seem extravagant to buy expensive riding clothes for children, especially when they grow so fast; always therefore make sure that there is a certain amount of room for alterations so that a jacket can be used for perhaps two seasons. There are always adverts for second-hand jackets in both *Horse and Hound* and the *BSPS News Review* – a reflection of the thriving second-hand market. I know of one lady who has a collection of BW jackets in store, which will allow her daughter to ride in style for many years in the future.

If you do not want the expense of visiting London for fittings, find a local tailor who may be able to make you a jacket for a third of the price. Remember however, that a riding jacket needs to be more skirted at the waist than an ordinary sports jacket, and slightly longer to cover the back of the saddle – and a bit longer still if your animal is long in the back. In the North, jackets that are too short are called 'bottom freezers'. The sleeves must also be a bit longer, as the arms are bent when riding: if when your arms are by your side, the sleeves are normal length or on the short side, then they will definitely be too short when riding, and will reveal too much shirt cuff which distracts the eye of the onlooker.

Some people are extremely lucky and can buy jackets off the peg; these can look just as good and usually work out cheaper than having them made up specially. Whether you do this or go to the expense of an exclusive tailor, make sure that your dress is correct for the occasion and a good fit – if you are not sure about correctness, go and watch some of the classes. Ill-fitting clothes are uncomfortable and do little for your confidence, which a showman must never lack. Do not make the excuse of a parent when buying a jacket a size too big that the child will grow into it; this may take a long time and in the interim the visual impression of pony and rider will have been spoilt. There was a boy who was very successful in WHP classes for many years who always wore a jacket which drowned him; at the beginning of every season people would remark that he was sure to have grown during the winter and that at last his jacket would fit – but for some strange reason his parents would always buy him another new jacket each season which was a size too big again!

All items of clothing and in particular jackets will last longer if looked after well – put them on a good solid coat-hanger when they are not being used, and brush them over well before putting them away in the wardrobe. Gloves and old numbers must not be left in the pockets otherwise they will leave the jacket mis-shapen.

Jodhpurs and Breeches

Since the advent of washable stretch material, it is a lot easier to find a well-fitting pair of jodhpurs or breeches which look very smart and are very comfortable to wear, especially on a hot day. Cavalry twill ones are hard wearing but can also be expensive and are less fashionable these days. On seeing an old picture of a lady judge wearing very hooped jodhpurs I enquired why she had such big pockets, and was told quite mischievously that it was where the judges put their packed lunches and bottles of gin on judging and hunting days! Over the last few years I have been extremely pleased with breeches made by Skin from Germany (formerly from Switzerland); this firm also makes the ski suits often seen on 'Ski Sunday'.

Off-white, cream or pale lemon are good traditional colours for the show ring; not white which belongs in the show-jumping world and certainly not luminous sulphur yellow which can make you look like an overweight canary or a bird of prey (praying that no-one will see you in them!). Always give new jodhpurs a good wash before wearing them so there is less chance of them slipping about in the saddle. Another good tip is to sew elastic on the bottom (coloured to match the boot) and fit it under the boot so that the jodhpurs will not ride up the leg, revealing the jockey's latest purchase from the Sock Shop! If you want to be very correct and copy the old-style breeches, you can sew on tiny buttons in the knee area to accommodate the boot straps; and remember to have the buckle of these straps on the outside centre of the knee, with the excess ends well tucked in (this also applies to spur straps).

Boots

Like a good jacket, a good pair of boots will last almost a lifetime and it is important that they fit well; not too tight so they make your legs swell up, nor too slack so you can get your hand down the side and your feet are moving about in the stirrups inside the boot; nor, as is so often seen, too short in the leg. If you are having boots made, make sure that they are long enough and come right to the base of the knee, which will allow for them to drop with wear.

A good pair of long boots made from quality leather are an expensive item, especially complete with trees, and if you are not prepared to pay vast amounts then I would advise you to look around for a good pair of second-hand ones. Occasionally you see a pair of Tom Hill or Maxwell boots for sale in *Horse and Hound*, when somebody has given up hunting. Shopping around for the best type of ready made, brand new ones is a good idea as quality can vary drastically, and the most expensive are not necessarily the best.

Make sure that your long boots are supple before going in the ring and if necessary, wear the new ones around the house to break them in; otherwise it will be like riding in a plaster cast, and it is the stiff boots which squeak every time you rise at the trot which can be very embarrassing. If your boots are a snug fit, nylon pop socks worn over jodhpurs or breeches will help you to put the boots on smoothly and will prevent the jodhpur riding up and wrinkling which can make your leg ache afterwards.

You will get good mileage out of your leather long boots if you look after them well. To quote Ronnie Marmont:

Take them off as soon as you have finished with them and put the trees in straightaway as opposed to walking around the show with them, or driving home with them or simply slinging them in the back of the Landrover without the trees. Wash them thoroughly with luke-warm water and let them dry naturally but not in front of direct heat like a fire. Wipe them down with methylated spirit. Make up a mixture of Kiwi polish and vinegar and bone this in the boot for five to ten minutes, and then get a polish using three types of brushes, shining them with a soft cloth.

Rubber riding boots are not altogether suitable, although they have a practical advantage in wet conditions and if a teenager has not stopped growing. The better quality ones can even look a bit like leather ones from a distance, and even more so if they are polished with ordinary boot polish and not 'Mr Sheen'!

The correct procedure is to wear spurs with long boots – though not in BSPS classes – even if these are dummy spurs and only for show. However, it is worth bearing in mind that judges do not wear them, and a horse which is used to them will often not go well for the judge because of this. Whatever you decide, and it is up to the individual situation, make sure that they fit properly and are clean, that they are the correct way up (facing down) and are not hanging at half-mast.

Dark tan jodhpur boots are preferable in pony classes – mine were in fact a lighter tan pair from Quant's of Newmarket; black ones are also smart but can look a little too formal on smaller feet. No matter what colour you choose, they should be clean and well polished if you don't want to look scruffy. The soles of new jodhpur boots are better rubbed with a matchbox to stop them slipping through the stirrups. Luckily we do not see the jodhpur boots with the straps and buckles much these days – these were unsightly and looked more like corrective footwear.

Collars and Ties

Nothing looks smarter at any time than a shirt with a good collar complemented by a silk tie with a small Windsor knot – simple and effective. So why do we see such scruffy alternatives in the ring? – short collars that curl up like British Rail sandwiches and meet below the Adam's apple (obviously mother has got the wrong neck size again), cuffs that sneak out from jacket cuffs and cover the hands (arm-bands would secure these) and ties that resemble unruly cravats. Not everyone can tie a good knot, so the ties on clips and elastic are ideal if this is the case.

Whatever tie you choose, make sure that it is pinned down and does not flap about when riding. Spotted ties are very popular – a more sober one for adults and brighter ones for the children, which can match the colour combination of the browband and so on. If you want to be a little more adventurous, a striped shirt with a white collar can look very professional; but do not be tempted to adopt the 'gangster look' by wearing a dark shirt and a very light tie, even if you think that it may intimidate the judge!

Some ladies are keen not to lose their femininity when wearing a shirt and tie; one of the nicest pictures to have been seen in the ring was when Susan Harper (daughter of the famous Scottish criminal lawyer Ross Harper) rode in a hack class, and as a contrast to her dark navy jacket wore a pale pink shirt with a pale pink tie, complemented by a small pink buttonhole.

Buttonholes

Buttonholes must be discreet and can add a dash of colour to the formality of riding wear, often matching the colour scheme of browbands, ribbons and ties. Above all avoid the large, tea-cup sized flowers with fern and silver paper which will make you look as though you are sponsored by Interflora! Remember it is a show class, not a wedding. Small buttonhole carnations, rosebuds and small cornflowers are quite acceptable in the showing classes as opposed to the hunter type ones. As a general guide, the rule should be that if you would not wear it in the hunting field, nor should you wear it in hunter classes.

With a buttonhole in the lapel, the flower will sit neatly if it is securely pinned from underneath; if there are no provisions in the lapel, remove the stalk and secure the flower head itself, pinning this from the underneath, face upwards. A fresh flower can give that final touch to the picture, although not everyone has time to go to the florist the day before the show – we buy a bunch of scarlet buttonhole carnations every week during the show season and put them in water which has liquid fertiliser in it; these will last a long time. Some people use artificial ones which can look like the real thing, though avoid plastic ones at all costs.

Accessories

Photographs of ponies in the 1950s depict jockeys with an endless number of badges on their jacket lapels, like girl guides or scouts; these badges could in fact have been dangerous if a jockey had fallen off. The same could be said about the present-day obsession for female riders to wear earrings when riding in the show ring – the less jewellery the better, and this also applies to the male population, whose flashy watches always seem to be on show.

A piece of cotton placed over the number will stop it billowing out, and will keep it flat. If the number is large, it can be cut down to a suitable size

Gloves

Wool and string gloves may look good in the hunting field and for everyday riding, but they look out of place in the modern-day show ring: leather or hogskin ones are far more popular, especially those which are unlined because they give more feeling of contact with the horse's mouth. In the rain, be careful that the dye doesn't run: I remember an eleven-year-old boy who looked like a heavy smoker because the dye had stained his hands light brown, and another young girl whose blue leather gloves ran in the rain and left her grey pony's shoulder a lovely pale blue colour – apparently it took a long time before this came out!

Leather gloves are in fact useless on wet days, because the wet reins become slippery and a rider can easily lose grip and ultimately control; the best type in these circumstances are the wool ones that have the rubber stipples on them and only cost about £2! Jockeys with bad hands are said to ride more sympathetically if they wear a few pairs of gloves – in theory, anyway!

Canes and Sticks

There are many types of show cane available these days; those with the silver top and end are expensive but make good presents, particularly with initials engraved on the head of the top. Canes are really for show only, but if they have to be dual purpose – if needed for a quick slap to wake the pony up – those with a flat side will not leave a mark on the pony's skin whereas the nomal type will. If a more practical type of stick is needed, say for working pony classes, the silver-topped ones with a flap at the end can be purchased. But remember, if ever a stick has to be used for correction, it is far more beneficial to give the pony a good solid 'thwack' just once, than to tap it umpteen times and make no impression whatsoever.

When choosing a show cane, pick one that matches the size of the rider – a professional showman will look silly with a lead-rein sized cane, just as a small 12.2hh rider will look unbalanced with a long cane. The long ones are usually carried by exhibitors who like to ride with one hand in horse classes, the cane being held in the free hand.

Some societies do not allow sticks over a particular length; for example, in all classes held under BSPS rules, whips must not exceed 30in (75cm) and exhibitors disobeying this rule will be disqualified. Hunting whips have become fashionable, especially in show hunter pony classes, and are quite permissible but must be complete to be correct. Just as these are fashionable, so the bamboo cane is considered unfashionable.

The long, swishing schooling whips belong at home, and not in the show ring; if they are needed on show day, then the schooling programme has gone astray somewhere along the line. These can be seen quite a lot in the in-hand classes, usually to chase up youngsters who as a result are too often seen with ears pinned back and tails swishing in temper. Schooling whips also leave quite noticeable weal marks.

Nothing beats a leather-covered cane for both in-hand and lead-rein showing (carried by the handler, not the jockey) – *not*, as I once saw, a piece of dirty alkathene pipe!

GENERAL STANDARDS

In general, the exhibitors who ride do make more of an effort to present themselves well, better than the in-hand people – apart from top people like David Ryde-Rogers in the pony classes and Ian Thomas (the Queen's dressmaker) in the hunter breeding classes. Some very untidy sights are seen in in-hand classes, except perhaps in the qualifying classes at the Ponies (UK) shows, such as the Colbeach and Risely championships where marks are given for turnout and presentation; because more of an effort has been made, some exhibitors are almost unrecognisable in their new attire.

It is sad, however, to think that this standard is not maintained at most of the other shows – the aim should be a high standard of turnout whether at a local show or Royal Windsor, particularly with the in-hand classes, because pony and handler are required to do so little to impress the judge, so something like presentation is extremely important. The picture of a well turned out young horse can easily be spoilt by a scruffy handler – and what is the point in that? – although it is certainly difficult to keep clean when plaiting tails and putting hoof-oil on foals. The secret is to leave getting yourself ready until the last minute.

Some well known in-hand exhibitors have made some items of clothing their trademark: Liz Mansfield often wears white wellingtons and the same head-scarf (for sentimental reasons, as it was bought the last time she showed Rotherwood Peepshow) and Andy Crofts always wears his cloth cap and black trousers.

Hats

The wearing of hats is not compulsory, although it is more correct at Wembley and suchlike; Mr R. Gilbert used to show many in-hand ponies for Miss Ferguson, and the only time I ever saw him wear a hat was at Wembley when he won with Rosevean Eagles Hill. Some exhibitors cannot cope with hats in windy conditions when showing in-hand and items of headgear can often be seen flying round the ring like UFOs.

In less blustery conditions, gentlemen handlers look good in a cloth cap with a tweed jacket, or in a bowler with a suit; the latter is more suitable at bigger shows and is mostly seen in hunter breeding classes. Trilbies really look better on spectators or when going into the ring to groom for somebody else; they can make some gentlemen handlers look like 'spivs' – and some of the wider-brimmed trilbies are quite ridiculous and make the handler look like a film extra from 'The Godfather'.

As with ridden classes, some people look better in different types of hat; this is especially so with the lady exhibitors in the in-hand classes. Some of them can look quite the part in a head-scarf, others look like Hilda Ogden. Some ladies look too masculine in trilbies and bowlers, and those that wear riding caps can look like riding instructors.

Footwear for Handlers

Sensible footwear is essential when running out in-hand animals, especially as some youngsters are clumsy and will often step on your toe by accident. The smart ladies who try to run in court shoes are very brave; I remember a few years ago when the conditions underfoot were atrocious – there was mud every-where, and a very well dressed lady lost her high heels during her individual show. Undaunted, she carried on as though nothing had happened and duly won her class, collecting her very smart footwear from the ring steward afterwards.

A well fitting jodhpur-type boot is perhaps preferable for running, rather than a shoe or a pair of clumsy wellingtons. Training shoes, although acceptable in mountain and moorland classes where dress is altogether a lot more relaxed and casual, are not really smart enough anywhere else. Exhibitors should wear comfortable practical clothes which are smart and clean and suit the occasion – the bigger the show, the more dressed up one can afford to be.

Turnout in General

The in-hand championship at Wembley is the climax of the year's in-hand showing, yet the varying standard of turnout always amazes me, even in the preliminary judging. Some people do make the effort – my brother and Colin Rose showed Ainsty Merry Maid and her foal wearing matching suits, yet others wear outfits which would be more suitable for painting and decorating! And again in the evening, only a few make the effort to dress up for the big occasion; trousers are hardly suitable for lady exhibitors at this stage, and they do look good in dresses – it is often the only time that their male colleagues get the chance to see their legs, and judging by their pale colour, some of them rarely see daylight anyway!

Gentlemen handlers should wear suits for the evening – Vin Toulson and Colin Rose even wore dinner suits one year with Twylands Title Page (without, I might add, the bowler hat and white pumps as sported by one gentleman one year, which did look rather strange!).

For the Lead-rein Class

Most horsey people are not fashion-conscious and prefer to adopt a smart, practical look rather than anything more ambitious. Very occasionally one sees a lady dressed to kill, and it is often when she is showing a lead-rein pony. Some of these handlers look as though they are dressed for a royal garden party, and often at the expense of the pony's turnout. Ronnie Marmont recalls judging a lead-rein class when a very smart lady in a daffodil silk outfit arrived in the ring, with a lovely pony and more particularly an enormous hat to match. When doing her individual show, the hat blew off and caused the pony to shy, and in consequence the rider fell off – unfortunately all, including the offending hat, had to retire. The moral of the story being: ladies, if you wish to display a David Shilling number, use a hat pin!

At the other end of the scale, some handlers look very untidy and their clothes have more hair on them than on the pony itself. Creating a pleasing picture is one of the major considerations of the lead-rein class and competition is very strong, so no stone should be left unturned. On many occasions ladies have made an effort to look smart, but that something special is just missing from the picture – perhaps the outfit is too dark and blends in too readily with a dark pony, or perhaps the outfit is simply not suitable. Those who have perfected the art of looking good in this class include Jocelyn Price (who used to show the famous Ready Token Pandora), Mary Ainscough (when showing Jilton Prince Charming) and more recently Linda O'Malley (showing Menai Prince Charming); a gentleman handler who is very successful in lead-rein presentation is Tony Asplin.

Men have less scope for dress than ladies and therefore less chance of going wrong, but there are nonetheless some comical sights. This usually arises from an overlarge bowler hat which rests on the handler's ears like a fruit bowl. Gentlemen look professional in a well fitting dark suit and bowler hat, and they can lessen the sombre impression by adding a light shirt and tie to match the colour combination of the whole turnout; a cane is not essential, but a good pair of gloves does much to finish the turnout. The look should be 'Sunday Best', not 'Saturday Night Fever'.

No matter what you wear, remember that the handler should tone into the background and complement the animal; for gentlemen particularly, the suit must fit well and the handler look elegant even when on the move, and lady handlers should wear sensible shoes – the show ring is not the place for high heels.

For the Side-saddle Class

Although I have produced the winning side-saddle pony at Royal Windsor Show on more than one occasion, I am certainly no expert – in fact, exercising this pony at home with a side-saddle was an ordeal! My advice would be to go to such people as Billet Mackie or Ronnie Marmont. Whether junior or adult, the overall picture should be one of elegance – it is amazing how often one sees the complete opposite! For instance, a habit should be well cut and should not show too much leg or the colour of the jodhpurs; then again, this does not mean that it should cover absolutely everything and have such a full skirt that it looks like something from 'Gone with the Wind'. Dark-coloured jodhpurs look more in keeping when the same colour habit is worn.

Fiona Benton-Jones riding Autumn Gem to win the Children's Side-saddle class at the Royal Show

Children look better in a riding cap or bowler (without a veil) and with a collar and tie – certainly not a silk hat, which is very much over-dressing. Adults should wear a bowler hat with a veil before noon, and to be correct, a top hat, veil and white hunting tie (more commonly, but incorrectly, known as a stock) after noon; hair should be tied back and formed into a bun, and sometimes a false one may be worn. Elegance will very soon be lost, however, if the jockey bounces about or slumps in the saddle like a bag of potatoes when on the move!

For Final Performances

Just as there is a strict code of etiquette when riding side-saddle, so there is for dress in the final performances at the major shows. Obviously if you are lucky enough to be chosen to go through for final judging you do want to look your best, and some people consider that going to the expense of having the correct clothes, even on the off-chance, is much better than having to beg, borrow and steal items of clothing from disappointed fellow competitors.

In hunter and cob classes, gentlemen are expected to wear full hunting dress, either the longer, skirted hunting coat or the Johnny Walker-style tail coat, complete with waistcoat and silk top hat, hunting tie and hunting whip. If a red coat is worn (not 'pink', which is the name of the tailor), white breeches with mahogany-topped boots and white garter straps would be the correct apparel. Ladies have an easier time, and need only a hunting tie (with a not-too-elaborate pin) and a top hat, although some do have a cut-away coat and linen waistcoat just for the occasion.

In the hack and riding horse classes, gentlemen should wear park dress, which consists of a black morning coat complete with black, close-fitting military trousers or overalls, with a collar and tie or cravat and waistcoat; the boots are called 'jemimas' and have a special spur fitted to them, though plain black jodhpur boots can be worn instead. A pair of pigskin gloves, a cane and a buttonhole will complete the outfit – this is one occasion when a man can wear a buttonhole, although it would not be appropriate with a swallow-tail coat in a riding horse class. In the more workmanlike riding horse class, some men wear tail coats but it is important to note that they do not carry hunting whips.

Looking and feeling the part in these circumstances gives one the confidence to ride brilliantly under the spotlight, which is the dream and ambition of so many.

Grooms must be suitably attired and exhibitors attentive in the line up

For the Groom

How a groom dresses for the ring is equally important – just as an untidy handler seems only too evident in the paddock when racing, so an untidy groom is noticed in the show ring. Dennis Coulton will not allow anyone in the ring unless smartly dressed and wearing a hat, and if only stewards at less significant shows would do the same it really would set a standard. Some firms actually offer prizes every so often to encourage this important aspect; Oakley Coachbuilders is one that immediately springs to mind.

IN SUMMARY

Whether you are an exhibitor – be it professional or amateur – a judge or steward, a rider or groom, your standard of dress reflects your attitude of mind and must be reasonable. Nobody is expected to look like a model from Vogue, just clean and tidy. If we do not do this we are letting down the horses we attend, our fellow exhibitors, the judges and the sport in general.

CHAPTER 8

Ringcraft

LEARNING THE TRADE

So much can be learned from observing others, and in this sport we are extremely lucky to be able to watch the experts perform each week at the big county shows during the summer – the way they gallop out of a corner, and the way in which they present the hacks so beautifully. These people have perfected their craft so they can earn a living; the show ring is their shop window and their talent is openly on display.

Whereas in other sports and hobbies the experts are often unapproachable and surrounded by a cordon of security, our professional showmen are far more accessible and human; providing you do not choose an inappropriate moment they will always lend a sympathetic ear and be happy to discuss any problems which you may be having with your horse. A professional showman has many jobs, and being a public relations officer is one of them; and if he is pleasant to you, it is more than likely that you will go back to him sometime in the future for a horse or for help with your schooling.

Advice and Tuition

In theory you will learn something from every horse or pony you deal with; it therefore follows that the professional who has many animals through his hands over the years will collect a wealth of experience – when you find yourself foxed by a particular problem, he might be able to solve it immediately. The moral is, never be afraid or too proud to take advice; people will think more of you for doing this, than if you make a mess of a horse because you thought you knew it all. All the top horsemen will tell you that they learn something new every day, and that even they will quite often go to someone for help or to brush up their

The author riding Brigand, Champion Hack at the Three Counties Show, 1984. A prolific winner in many spheres, Brigand had been evented before being shown as a small, lightweight and working hunter, in hack classes, and finally as a riding horse

150

Nigel Hollings riding Super Coin (right), reserve to Vin Toulson and Elite (left) at Shrewsbury in 1983. These two finished in the same order in the Waterford Crystal Hunter Points Championship that season

riding, which surprises most amateurs. I visited one of our top riders during the Christmas holidays one year and having arrived slightly early, watched her going through a gruelling lesson given by one of the people who worked for her and who had been a past student of hers.

Juniors often benefit more from outside tuition because – as with driving lessons – parents are not always the best instructors; they are too emotionally involved, which can result in frayed tempers all round. Besides, outside opinion can sometimes suggest that vital missing ingredient which you are unable to see because you are so much involved; and never laugh at even the opinion of a non-horsey friend, because at times someone such as he can hit the nail on the head, so to speak, in his ignorance.

When producing ridden animals, help will often be needed from the ground whilst you are riding, as showing is very much a visual activity; besides which, all horses must learn to go for riders other than yourself so it pays to put up friends of different size, weight and ability on each of your animals every so often.

Showmanship

The top showman will have a certain flair, and an air of competence about him as well as a sense of theatre; he will make even the most difficult horse look comfortable, and the plainest of horses look a star – yet he will never allow himself to overshadow the horse, but will present the exhibit to the best of his ability by performing with it as a partnership. By knowing each horse's faults and shortcomings he will be able to cover up these deficiencies, yet will make the most of the good points such as a good gallop, or a good straight movement when trotting out in hand. These people will know more about the horse than the judge ever will because of the time factor, and this is often why a professional will sometimes describe as his best horse, surprisingly, an animal which has only had moderate success in the ring.

Appropriate Classes

One of the reasons that some top show exhibits do not reach their full potential – apart from bad production – is because they have not had appropriate classes chosen for them, nor been placed under the right judge. This is an important aspect of indirect ringcraft – after all, the show animal relies on the producer who must give him the best possible chance of success, just as the actor depends on his agent. If an animal is only second-rate yet remains unbeaten for a while, the prestige it will gain as a result is considerable; but even if your animal is top class, if it is entered in unsuitable classes and is beaten on its first few outings, it will lose credibility despite its quality. Some people will say that a good animal will win under any judge but unfortunately, and for whatever reason, this does not always happen. History shows that there is always one judge who wants to make a name for himself and be the first one to put a champion down. Pretty Polly, Pollyanna and Holly of Spring were all beaten.

More usually, owners are sometimes not aware of a judge's preference, and put their potential star under a judge who will either simply not like the type, or will not appreciate the way it goes in preference to, say, its less spectacular conformation. The top showman must see that this possibility is lessened, and does get to know over the years what a particular judge will go for.

Those judges who change their priorities and opinions every couple of seasons are the most difficult to please and show under. Again, this is a subject that a professional would help you with, rather than your so-called best friend who will sometimes guide you up the wrong path – whether deliberately or by accident. There are inevitably some rogues in the circus of professionals, but on the whole they will give you an honest opinion and answer.

Jockeyship

In pony classes there are supposed to be no professional riders, just children, as one mother told me – how wrong she is! In pony classes in particular the jockey can be the all-deciding factor as to whether an animal succeeds or 'just misses the ticket', and in fact a skilled jockey with showmanship can easily beat a less competent rider even though on a better pony. This professional-ism comes with experience; when teaching young jockeys at home, there comes a point in the training where nothing can beat practical experience, and only by making mistakes in the ring can the person learn anything further. Smaller shows rather than the big county shows are ideal to start with, where a jockey can put theory taught at home into practice – even if it is only a best rider or handy pony class.

For a jockey learning the tricks of the trade, a schoolmaster-type show animal is a must at some point in his or her career, and possibly again if, for example, the show pony jockey decides to go into WHP classes and needs to be educated over fences; and yet again when the transition from ponies to horses is made. So much progress can be made once a rider has become confident – confidence will enable him to pull out all the stops when necessary, which is something a timid jockey will never do.

It is vital to match the pony with the rider, or vice-versa, to produce the perfect picture which performs well together. Too many parents buy a champion pony regardless of whether the jockey will cope with it or look good on it. Another point to remember is that when showing in hand, a tall person can make an animal look small, and a small person can make an animal look very big – something to be aware of when trying to create a certain illusion.

Novice Ponies

Even though the novice pony may have been shown in hand, he will often benefit from going to shows just to ride round, to allow him to absorb the atmosphere and see the sights. Similarly a novice jockey can gain a lot of experience by competing in equitation classes at smaller shows. Some people will take the pony to a show as a spectator for a full season, which is admirable if you can afford to do it. People who scoff at this are often those owners whose ponies only last a couple of seasons because they have been over-produced when they are neither mentally nor physically ready; as compared to ponies which have been given time, and are consequently still winning in the ring in their early teens.

Rules and Regulations

If showing novice ponies at small fun shows, make sure that they have no chance of de-novicing by accident. Part of the showman's job is to know the rules and regulations backwards, so as to avoid an infringement – for example, showing a horse in both a hunter class and a riding horse class on the same day is not allowed at most affiliated shows; nor is showing a pony which the judge may have had dealing with; and so on.

When selling a pony, make sure that all relevant information such as this is given to the new owners, to avoid the risk of their entering a class and travelling hundreds of miles to discover, when it is too late, that the pony must only be withdrawn. This is so often the case at shows; and although the onus is on the exhibitor simply because the judge will probably not recognise the animal – possibly having sold it as a foal – it is still very annoying for this to happen to anybody.

Similarly, if a show changes judge, exhibitors must be

informed; some shows do this, and refund the entry fee when necessary. If a judge who has had a connection with any of our horses is officiating at either RIHS or HOYS, we still enter just in case that judge is unable to attend at the last minute, partly because we have gone to the trouble of qualifying for these. For example, we entered Runnings Park Hill Star for the RIHS in 1988 even though Jennifer Williams was judging – she had had a connection with him, having looked after him as a weaned foal; this was just in case – especially as he always went well at Birmingham, having been reserve champion in 1986 and champion in 1987.

SHOW DAY

On approaching the showfield make sure that you are displaying the correct gate pass; this will be of assistance to yourself and any policemen or gatemen on traffic duty. And to save some time when arriving at the appropriate entrance, have all the relevant documents handy: 'flu cards, height certificates if necessary, and make sure that health certificates are signed. Always read the literature when it comes in the post, even if it is several weeks before the show, to check that the judges and the times are the same, and in particular make a note of what times the gates open and close to exhibitors – there is nothing worse than arriving at the showground to find the gates locked. Though what happened at Wembley last year was almost as bad – the vet was not on duty to check 'flu cards until an hour before the first class, and the 12.2hh ponies were not allowed to be unloaded until checked, which caused an uproar.

An Overnight Stay
If arriving at the show the night before, check in with the horse foreman, and then the first consideration is to prepare the stables; in particular look in the manger and remove any old food left by the previous inmate, because the first thing a pony usually does is to investigate the manger when it goes into a new stable. When mucking out, put the wet straw at the end of the horsebox lines rather than dumping it outside the door; working round these piles the next day can be very unpleasant, especially if the weather is hot.

It is better to erect tarpaulin sheets whilst the stables are empty; there will be less risk of frightening the horses while you climb about along the front of your stables. Your object, especially if it is dark on arrival, is to get the horses settled as soon as possible so that they can have a feed at least once before settling down for the night.

If feeding cut grass make sure that it is cool, otherwise it can cause colic. We always carry a torch in the lorry, which is an essential piece of equipment when stabling overnight – I have forgotten the number of times I have plaited by torchlight!

The Plan of Campaign

Unless we have an exceptionally sharp horse, we do not often exercise the animals on the showground the night before the show, but instead allow them to unwind after the journey. If you arrive at the show as we do, in the morning, it is wise to have some sort of plan of campaign; work out the timetable, sorting out when each animal must be ready – important issues like human meal times must be put to the back of your mind, and the horses definitely take priority.

Everybody who travels to the show with us is acquainted with the plan of events; this is essential if competing in more than one ring at a time, which of course can be subject to last minute changes depending on the judge and the entries. For example, if I am riding a horse in the main ring it is impossible for me to take charge of an animal in Ring 2 at the same time, so a competent member of the team will do this independently. This is another reason for educating a jockey to think for himself, so that he can compete without several members of the family or yard shouting instructions from every corner of the ring; this is all too common a practice these days.

One top trainer heard that an ex-pupil of hers was setting up a showing stable of her own, and said without prevarication that this would not work because the girl would not even canter in the ring without instruction, couldn't think for herself and consequently had not learnt as much as she could have done. With the exception of the tiny tot jockeys, we have always made an effort to educate our jockeys so this sort of situation will not happen to them – after all, what better advert for a trainer than if his ex-pupils go into the wide world and make a name for themselves?

Late Entries and Substitutions

On arrival, send someone to collect the numbers and make sure that if there is any money to pay for late entries that the debt is settled before competing. There have been occasions where public pressure has forced a show secretary to change her mind about accepting an entry not listed in a catalogue, even though it had been accepted over the telephone the night before. However, once the secretary has received money, it is virtually impossible for this sort of thing to happen.

Due to the strict substitution rules, if ever you wish to change an entry and the secretary is agreeable, always make a point of paying the additional entry fee. A kind-hearted secretary, thinking to save you money, may automatically substitute the entry for you, but obviously does not realise the trouble she can involve you in. The BSPS has banned some exhibitors in the past for substituting an entry simply because this can cause administration difficulties if the 'wrong' pony has qualified for Peterborough, and is not the one on the secretary's form which goes to the BSPS office. We very seldom buy a catalogue, unlike others who want to know who is entered in their class as soon as they arrive on the showfield. The way entries are these days, this is often pointless as the whole world appears to be entered.

THE SHOW ATMOSPHERE

If your animal has been schooled properly and prepared well at home, the working-in procedure at a show is a mere formality. Obviously some animals need more work than others, and they all respond to the show atmosphere differently – some become whirling dervishes as soon as their feet touch the showfield, others adopt a facial expression which says it all – 'Not another show!' There are people who arrive at the showground intending to complete their schooling and in the hope that all the movements which have not been achieved at home will fit into place once on the showfield; they are only kidding themselves. It has to be said, however, that there are some animals who do not look at all like show animals at home in work, but do enjoy being in the show ring and rise to the occasion.

Getting the working-in procedure right is a very exacting task indeed, and the close understanding you have with your horse plays a vital part. Not enough work can make your animal's chances in the ring short-lived, just as too much work before the competition can take the edge off him and give the judge a very boring impression. Again this is where the experienced showman will win the day – he will have learned from experience exactly how much work is needed and how competent the judge is; whether she will want to be taken or whether she will want a steady, sluggish ride.

Horses which have been produced several times for the ring usually behave consistently when on a showfield and are the easiest to prepare for the ring; unlike the novice, who within a short space of time can go from one extreme to the other, often as a result of nerves. If your jockey is competent it is better to have a novice a little 'flat' (rather than over-sharp) on its first few appearances, to avoid any traumas in the ring as these tend to remain in the mind of the more intelligent show animal, especially a mare, for a long time.

Once a novice is relaxed and at home both in the ring and amongst the flags and tradestands, he should gain in confidence over a gradual period of time and develop well. The judge will often forgive a young animal a certain amount of greenness when competing against older animals (providing the right basic ingredients are there) and so it does not need to operate like the Pony of the Year straightaway.

There are some show animals that work in well and are still relaxed in the collecting ring, but when they enter the ring they adopt a split personality and start to boil; this is the worst type of animal to produce because you never know where you are. Any horse can be expected to light up a little when surrounded by other horses, though this is something they should have been accustomed to at home if produced properly, but some animals change the minute they enter the ring and start to swish their tails and generally throw away their chances from the very start. This is often because in the past they have been badly ridden when in the ring, and have taken advantage of their rider on previous occasions. Those judges who will keep such an animal in the class even though it cannot possibly be placed are to be admired, otherwise the pony in question may get the impression that every time it is naughty it is taken out of the ring, and this is something which should not be encouraged. Sometimes an exhibitor will be given the option by the judge and will ask to remain in the class for this very reason.

Some shows are far more electrifying than others, and when entering a busy show it may not be worth taking a pony which quickly hots up in noisy conditions. Shows will swap rings, though, from time to time, so it pays to look at the schedule very carefully. For instance, at one particular show the ring was deceivingly electric and although reasonably peaceful, a lot of ponies used to go badly in it; we stopped taking one particular pony, and in fact stopped asking for a schedule – only to discover that the rings had been moved around and that for two seasons the ponies had been shown in a quiet backwater of the showground which would have suited our pony much better.

Ponies will nearly always go better in some rings rather than others – Gay Sovereign obviously liked the Great Yorkshire main ring and particularly excelled himself in the Peterborough main ring, where he won the 14.2hh class at the BSPS Championships on at least five occasions. On the other hand, another successful 14.2hh pony would always become upset by aircraft noises, so we would avoid those showfields which were next door to an airfield, such as Ayr and the Royal Highland.

With entries so big in classes these days, some shows will split a class into two sections and this can cause even further problems when working in. Then you have to decide whether to have your animal worked in properly for the section at the risk of him being flat for the final (if he is lucky enough to be chosen), or whether to send him into the preliminary judging sharp and risk him exploding, in the hope that he makes it to the final when he will still have enough spirit to perform really well.

THE PRELIMINARIES

On Arrival
Some animals benefit from being grazed for a while when arriving at a show, especially those that tuck up when travelling and obviously need a little time to relax. One of the funniest photographs I have seen taken at a showground is of a show rider grazing his horse and reading a paper at the same time; on the fence there is a notice saying 'Beware of pickpockets' – and on closer inspection the horse can be seen lifting something, all unbeknown, from the rider's jacket pocket!

Working In
If the horse needs only a leg-stretch rather than faster work, just lead him about, though if he is plaited, remember that plaits may be damaged if he stretches whilst grazing, and to be safe use a lunge line just in case he takes fright. Better still, ride him around the showground on a sort of hack. If an animal, particularly a youngster, needs 'setting up' it can be walked around 'in tack'.

Sometimes these well-drained showgrounds are rock hard in summer, so walking exercise is all that you dare give some animals. The Royal Show has good working-in facilities, including two all-weather schools; other showgrounds, like Devon County, have hardly any facilities at all.

If older animals need a lot of work, they can be lunged for a while rather than ridden for a very long time – a horse's back will get sore if it is ridden hard for any length of time. However, when on the lunge, make them work hard and don't let them just amble about; but do not chase them around at breakneck speed as some people do in the hope of tiring them out, as there is more chance of laming them by doing this. We also alternate riding and lungeing with some horses, and often give an animal a quiet spin on the lunge with the show tack on just before entering the ring to get his back down (a good idea with novice ponies) and to check if he has got his second wind.

Normal working-in procedures vary but have a common aim: to have a relaxed, supple and obedient horse when going into the ring. A short, sharp gallop can sometimes do wonders to get a horse's back down and give him a good 'pipe opener', although this can excite some horses too much and encourage them to take too strong a hold in the class. Once at Ayr show, an exhibitor thought it would be a good idea to take his show hunter around the race track as a way of giving him some work before the class, but made the mistake of getting carried away and overdoing the galloping – the horse stiffened up as if it had azoturia, and was thus unable to compete.

A lot of juniors can often be seen galloping their show hunter ponies around the showfield on baked ground in an effort to impress their friends. Riders should realise that this sort of exhibition riding often leaves ponies with rounded joints, or worse still, lame. It is therefore much better to exercise sensibly in some quiet corner of the showfield, asking the animal for bends and practising transitions, and performing suppling exercises just as you would at home. When you are quite happy that he is going consistently well, he has probably done enough; make sure that he has cooled down properly before taking him back to the box to be got ready.

If exercising in and out of horsebox lines, be careful of people opening doors and of horses coming down ramps, and of course watch out for moving vehicles. On some showfields this is unfortunately very often the only area available for working in.

Always allow enough time for your horse to receive the finishing touches, and for you to get changed into your showing clothes. Of course, there are some animals which can be shown without any working in at all – people who own a pony which will come into the ring virtually straight off the horsebox are really to be envied!

Be very careful when working in amongst horse boxes

Showing Indoors

When showing indoors at the beginning of the season the space allowed for working in is usually extremely restricted; we will very often do the working in at home so that only a little needs to be done at the show. The golden rule when riding in a restricted area is to ride right shoulder to right shoulder to avoid any crashes with oncoming ponies.

If you intend to show on the indoor circuit, take your horse to your local indoor school first for a practice before your first outing. Indoor showing is useful during the months when the weather is bad and unpredictable, but can hardly be considered as a practice for the outdoor shows – they are so different, in atmosphere and space and in so many ways, although admittedly some of today's indoor arenas are bigger than some of the rings at an outdoor show.

In the Collecting Ring

Before going into the main ring, it is a good idea to spend some time in the collecting ring to accustom your horse to the

162

atmosphere and the other horses. What you do depends on your horse – you may be better just walking round, making him work into his bridle; maybe he needs some faster work to warm him up for the class; if he is one which 'stews up' easily in a new environment, you may be better going straight into the ring from the stable area. This is also a good time to size up the competition in your class; and if you are in the second section of a class, you can watch the final placings of the first and it may give you an idea of what the judge is going for. Do some last minute checks such as on girth straps, stirrup leathers and keepers on bridles.

IN THE RING

When entering the ring, leave a good space in front of you and go behind something which will make your animal look special; do not go directly behind an animal which is, say, a better walker than yours or has got more presence thus making an unfavourable comparison early on. Enter the ring at walk – it used to be the fashion for the whole class to charge into the ring like a street scene from 'West Side Story', but this is gradually being stopped by some senior stewards at the request of many of the judges at the bigger shows. Treat the ring as a theatre: when you pass in front of the judge you are on stage for several seconds, so have your performance just right, whereas behind him/her you are backstage and you can perform more last minute checks such as sitting trot or half-halts – if the judge is worth his salt he should only watch one side, just occasionally casting a glance behind if necessary; some judges miss most of the exhibits because they will insist on following only a few ponies around the ring. When in front of the judge for the first time some showmen acknowledge him/her by nodding or touching their hat; this can be overdone at times and simply causes the judge to smile or squirm, but with equal indifference.

First Impressions

First impressions are long lasting, so make sure that your horse is walking out well, on the bridle, and ears forward; some very strange noises can often be heard coming from the rider, like a click or a whistle, in an effort to make the horse prick its ears – one top showman blows raspberries which can be very off-putting! The walk is one of the most difficult paces to get right, especially if the horse is not a 'natural' – the 'natural' will walk into a ring with majestic splendour, as if to say 'look at me', with his tail cocked and swinging like a metronome, and is a rare sight indeed. So often the walk is too fast or too slow, and this is not a good basis from which to move up through the paces.

Finding a Space

One of the most important aspects of ringcraft is to find and keep a space so that your horse can move smoothly and calmly, and therefore give the judge, who after all is the main person to impress, more of an opportunity to see you – which he won't be able to if you are hidden in a bunch. This often happens in children's classes, where a lone rider is to be seen on one side of the ring and a cavalry charge on the other. If your horse is being slowed down by the one in front there are many ways to achieve more room: by half-halting, thus allowing the animal in front a wider berth; by circling into a space behind you; or by overtaking at trot across the ring into a healthier gap.

Sometimes finding a space is taken to an extreme, however, usually by novice exhibitors whose sole ambition seems to be to find a niche even at the expense of showing off the horse properly – he can be seen twirling in circles like a dancer in 'Swan Lake', misjudging the timing and cutting off the other exhibitors in mid-stream and in fact being a total menace to everyone concerned. It is because of this that some stewards will not allow exhibitors to overtake – which in any case is extremely bad manners if it is done in front of the judge; this can be a bind, however, if the horse in front is extremely naughty, or is short-striding and perhaps slower altogether. In this situation the only course open to you is to half-halt and go deep into the corners thus creating a slight, if only temporary gap; although if everyone did this, it would soon look like a car 'pile-up' backstage.

THE PACES

Trot

As well as casting a glance towards the judge to see what is happening, you must also keep an eye on the stewards who are basically there to see that everyone gets a fair crack of the whip by ensuring that the class runs smoothly. Be alert for when the steward sends you into trot, as this will soon sort out the wheat from the chaff; if your horse excels at this pace, make the most of it – but do not make the mistake of trotting too fast so that the horse is unbalanced and on his forehand. If you know your horse is likely to do this, do some sitting trot just before you go 'on stage' to collect him.

As you ride up through the gears and the pace becomes faster, so you must keep your wits about you and judge spaces and distances a lot more accurately, as well as concentrate more on your riding. Sometimes an exhibitor – and this includes one or two of our top professionals – will anticipate the move into canter, especially if his mount does not go particularly well in trot, and of course the rest of the class, not wanting to fall for the 'last-one-is-a-cissy' situation, follow on like sheep. This is when you see if your steward is in command – more often than not he is quite baffled and will allow the proceedings to continue.

Canter

When officially told or asked to canter – depending on your steward – wait until you reach a corner, especially with a young pony, and prepare the transition correctly and smoothly. If you become flustered and allow the pony to run through the movement it could take you half the ring to have him back between hand and leg, and then of course you run the risk of going on the wrong leg – much better to trip into canter and then ask him for more pace so that you can maintain the correct shape; quite apart from the fact that it looks more pleasing to the judge.

If you do go on the wrong leg, keep your composure and try to rectify the situation as soon as possible; if there is a strong chance of this happening again, wait until you are backstage. The canter should be smooth and collected in pony and hack classes, whereas in hunter and cob classes the canter can be more workmanlike, covering the ground in readiness for the gallop.

The Gallop

In BSPS classes, 15hh and 15.2hh animals can be galloped together, as is the case in WHP and SHP championships. When galloping, the theatre analogy is even more relevant: there is no need to fly round the ring like 'Evil Knevil' trying to break a track record – instead, pick up momentum backstage, and when about to pass in front of the judge, glide on, coming out of the first corner balanced and meaning business and steadying up in the second – the judge is looking to see a lengthening of stride rather than a shuffle, with a certain degree of control.

Changing the Rein

If and when you are asked to change the rein, look ahead for a

Find a suitable space, and keep a watchful eye on both judge and steward; it is a sin to miss your cue

line and plan where you are going to try and ask for left-rein canter; the change should be smooth and precise, and if wrong legs are again a problem, wait for the left bend. If on a novice, give him plenty of room and do not go too close or get boxed in by animals approaching on the opposite rein. Judges will be looking to see if animals go as correctly on the other rein, and will sometimes ask ponies to remain at trot for a while before making a left-rein canter.

The Initial Line-Up
When asked to walk, make the transition smooth, and walk into a suitable space, keeping a watchful eye on both judge and steward who will hopefully call you up into line – it is a sin to miss your cue. At this stage the set can look like a scene from a cowboy film with the jockeys circling the judge like Red Indians. If you are not chosen straightaway, do not lose hope – remember that the class is only a quarter of the way through at this stage, and that this judgement is only a matter of initial choice.

Once in line, keep your animal attentive but relaxed, especially when the judge inspects the line-up – like soldiers on parade. Some exhibitors seem to think that once in line they have reached a sanctuary; however, the line-up is not a church rest-tent and it pays to look smart, particularly as the judge will often cast a glance at the line-up during the class to confirm his/her ideas – if found slouching, it could cost you a placing or two.

Leave enough space between you and your neighbours so that the judge can walk in between; besides which, if ponies are too close to each other they may start to feel uneasy and move about, and very often it is the innocent party which is ordered out of the ring by the judge for 'not standing in line'. This happened to me at the RIHS one year; I was pulled in third, with a good chance of moving up to top until the two ponies above me started messing about and pushed my pony. The judge turned round and acted immediately on what she thought were the top three ponies behaving badly and put all of us into the back line – I was not pleased! However, situations often balance themselves out in the show ring – I have been lucky to win classes on animals which, unbeknown to the judge, have upset the line-up!

THE INDIVIDUAL SHOW

Many people dread the individual show most of all, although I cannot understand why – at least you can concentrate on the job in hand rather than having to worry about other competitors getting in your way and you also know that the judge is watching you, or should be; judges who turn their backs on a competitor doing an individual show to talk to the stewards are truly appalling – surely this can be done whilst watching?

Before starting your show and perhaps whilst watching other competitors, you should work out what shape your show is going to take. There should always be basic pattern and sequence of transitions – it is better to keep the content simple and effective than to try to be clever and make a real mess.

Nonetheless, if your horse is capable of that extra something or the situation dictates that you have to pull out all the stops, say in a championship, then certainly you must go for it. I remember a hack class at the East of England a few years ago when I was riding Brigand, and the first few competitors had all tried to outdo each other; the atmosphere was extremely competitive. Brigand, who was pulled in second, excelled at changing legs at canter so at the end of my show following a rein-back to canter, I came along the front changing legs at every other stride – needless to say, he won the class. However, because I was concentrating so much, I finished the show by halting in front of the next competitor who was waiting to come out of line; this happened to be Davina Whiteman who said in a rather sarcastic tone: 'Thank you, Nigel dear'!

At this crucial time you should make the most of your animal – do an extra trot if it is sensational at this pace, or make the most of a gallop if it has an exceptional top gear. It is also commonsense that if your pony anticipates his show, do something different to confuse him.

A few years ago in the pony championship at Wembley, the two judges – the late Mrs A. Clerke-Brown and Peter Brookshaw – couldn't agree between the 13.2hh (Holly of Spring) and the 14.2hh (Solway Redwood), both winners and competing for champion. The referee, who was Jennifer Williams, was called in and both jockeys rode brilliantly, making full use of their ponies' good paces – Holly had an exquisite trot and did very little else in the show and Redwood had a very elegant canter and did many figures of eight. The former stole the limelight on this occasion, and in fact won the Wembley title for four consecutive years.

When performing an individual display there are certain points to remember. If a judge specifically asks for a certain show or insists on a quick, sharp show – do exactly that. Use every inch of the ring and take your time – you are not in a speed class. However, do not bore the judge by doing too long a show. Have your transitions smooth and keep the turns flowing, especially in the figures of eight which should be symmetrical. When changing the rein in canter, trot for no more than four strides before asking for canter on the other leg; if you trot too early it looks like a first-ridden show, and if left too late it looks as though you are using the ropes on the ring-side for braking.

When extending at canter or galloping, lengthen the stride gradually, and be sure to come back to hand just as smoothly – the one should not look like a spontaneous charge, nor the other like a car running out of petrol. Also, as much attention should be paid to the closing stages of an individual show as to the beginning – after all, it is the last thing a judge sees. If you make a mistake early in the show, it may well be forgotten if you finish well. However, if you start a show nicely but then it gradually deteriorates towards the end, this will not be forgotten so easily.

Halt in front of the judge a reasonable distance away so that he/she can memorise a clear picture – don't get so close that all they can see is their reflection in your boots, or too far away so that they need binoculars. It pays to be able to rein back if so required by the judge in a pony class – the championship at Devon County one year was decided simply on this movement. It is expected in hack classes, where the content of the show should be a little more ambitious.

The fashion these days seems to be to throw the reins down at the end of the show or to pat with noisy effusion; it all looks very calculated, and is really quite incongruous if the pony has been very naughty. Similarly, if a show rider is going to make the effort to smile while in the ring, to transmit to the judge that it is a real pleasure to be riding such a top class horse – then make sure it looks natural. Some of our young female jockeys look positively fiendish with their plastic grins!

A good jockey must be sharp enough to alter a show midstream so as to avoid unexpected hazards such as a paper bag being blown across the ring, or a straying dog (one year at the RIHS a garden shed was actually moved about the ring while the large hacks were doing their individual displays). It looks tidier to have the loops of your reins on the outside of the pony's shoulder, and it looks professional if you flick the flap of your jacket over the cantle of the saddle at regular intervals during the class, particularly when waiting in front of the judge at the beginning of the show and especially if your pony is long in the back.

THE JUDGE'S RIDE

When it is the judge's turn to ride your horse, have the stirrups the right length; if the steward has not already done this for you, you can check the length with a horse he has already ridden. Be available to assist the judge in getting on board either by holding the horse, or holding the stirrup on the offside, or by giving a leg up. The judge may wish to mount by himself and the horse should have been trained to stand still so that he does not move off from the line-up until asked. If he is prone to fidget in line

Help the judge, and keep chat down to a bare minimum

when unmounted, or if his back comes up when mounted after a short rest, it is better to stay on board until the very last minute before the judge arrives.

Do not get into a lengthy conversation with the judge, a simple 'good morning' will suffice; certainly not a life history of the horse or a detailed account of how to ride it. When it is returned, say 'thank you', and do not give an opinion of how the judge has ridden it. Top class judges know when someone is trying to creep and can at times easily take offence. Simply be polite and courteous and helpful, making sure that the reins or the stirrup irons are not twisted, and if it is raining make sure that the saddle is dry before the judge sits on it.

THE IN-HAND PHASE

The next stage is for your groom to clean up the horse for the in-hand phase. It is amazing how trends have changed; years ago, only a stable rubber and a body brush were taken into the ring – nowadays, grooms almost need an assistant themselves to carry the show boxes – which look like 'portaloos' – the buckets, the rugs and so on and so forth. Many a class has been won or lost on the in-hand show, and this is something which should have been perfected at home. Some judges can be very strict and award a high percentage of the marks for this phase; others prefer the way of going to be a priority with the conformation stage a formality. Either way, some jockeys seem to think that the in-hand phase is easy, and make mistakes through not trying; this is particularly noticeable in WHP classes.

Look for a suitable patch of ground on which to stand your horse, either level or slightly up-hill, but never down-hill, and make sure that your animal has not fallen asleep in line before he comes out in front of the judge. If possible you want to be facing in the direction in which you are going to walk away; you will have a better chance of finding a straight line and can avoid any unnecessary tight turns. In the last few strides as you stand the pony up, try to be accurate with the feet – the judge hasn't got all day for you to fluster about, pushing and pulling the animal for a couple of minutes or more.

If the judge is looking from the nearside, then the nearside legs want to be furthest apart so that he is looking at the picture 'in the frame' so to speak. When he moves to the other side, have the offside legs furthest apart either by moving the pony back or forwards a stride. Whichever side the judge is looking from, do not stand alongside the animal but in front, so that he can see the pony's head clearly. Work out at home whether the pony looks better for having a high head carriage or a long and low one in the in-hand phase. Often jockeys throw grass in the air which results in the pony looking skywards, revealing an ugly underneath neck muscle. Similarly, too low a head carriage can make the pony look like a dinosaur!

If there are two judges, always present the pony to the senior judge, and failing that the female judge, though do make sure that you don't favour the probationary one by mistake. When you walk away from him, you must try to keep in a straight line, so focus on something at the ring-side and keep the strides even. Turn left off your track and then back on the same line at a nice steady, balanced trot – not too fast which is so often seen – and keep going until behind the line-up. If this is done well there should be no reason for having to do it again, unless the judge thinks that your pony is lame – which can happen easily if ponies knock themselves because they are turned and twisted quickly in an in-hand show.

1

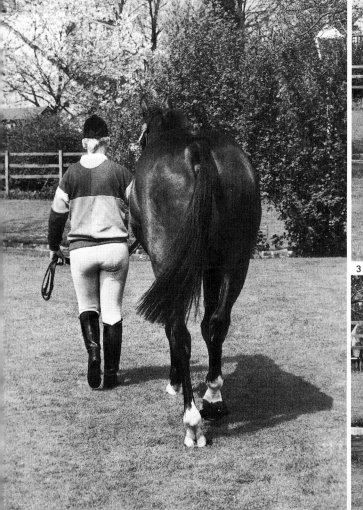

2

3

Showing in-hand
(Far left) When the judge is examining the horse from the nearside, the nearside legs should be further apart from those on the offside
(Left) How not to do it! This horse is standing incorrectly for the judge, who is viewing from the nearside. The handler should be standing in front of the horse

(Below) Walk away from the judge in a straight line, keeping the strides even (1) Turn left off the track (2), and then back on the same line (3) . . . at a nice, steady trot (4)

4

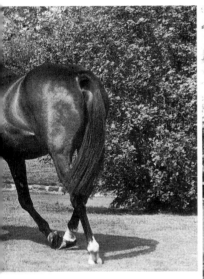

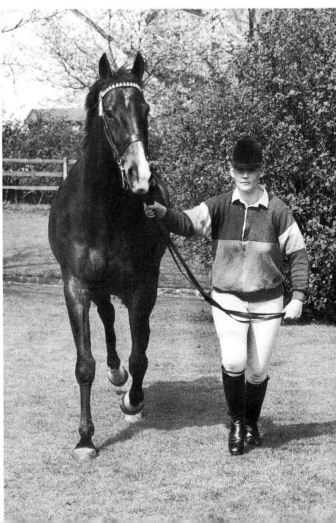

Remember to keep the pony's head straight when showing in-hand

If you need more practice, enter in-hand classes at some smaller shows. Always remember to keep the pony's head straight and not turned in towards you, which from the judge's viewpoint will make the pony look short of front. When giving your initial trot round the ring from halt, walk a few strides before you start to trot, keeping the pony up to his bridle to achieve maximum balance, and gradually allowing the pony's head to relax whilst moving on; above all, try to come down to walk just as smoothly. Even though in-hand showing doesn't seem as demanding as the ridden job, there is much to learn to perfect its technique.

THE FINAL JUDGING

Once your saddle is back on again, you can either remount straightaway or leave it until the last minute, depending on your horse. Once mounted, it may be as well to have a quick walk round at the back of the line so that the girth can be tightened up gradually and whilst making sure that the horse's back is down; if you tighten it whilst standing in line, you may find that he has a bucking fit on leaving the line-up for the final walk round.

At no other stage in the proceedings is a good balanced walk more important; the judge may even ask the class to trot again, which is a good enough reason to have the horse between your hand and leg before you walk off. But remember: no matter where you are placed, the animal is the same individual and it is the opinion of that judge on that particular day. And when receiving the all-important rosette – no matter what its colour – *always* be polite; showing is a small world and even if you do not agree with your placing you may have to go under that same judge another time. If you fall out with certain judges on a regular basis and vow never to go under them again, you may find that in a very short space of time you are grounded at home for most of the season.

THE LAP OF HONOUR

Proceedings are over when the steward dismisses the class; until this actually happens, if an animal misbehaves the judge is perfectly entitled to remove any rosette – this can be particularly distressing in children's classes. It is remarkable how many well behaved animals perform badly on their lap of honour; many of the jockeys simply do not bother because the class is finished, which is stupid because with some judges this could affect the decision of the championship, even though this should in fact be judged as a separate class. If left uncorrected, this type of high spirits could lead to other bad habits and problems such as bolting out of the ring; quite apart from the fact that it may make the judge look a fool. Just as you walk into a ring at the start of the class so should you leave the ring at walk.

At no time must you show any resentment to people who have beaten you; always offer them a word of congratulation, otherwise you will build up a reputation for being a bad sport.

We always analyse the classes and placings on the way home in the privacy of the horsebox, and sometimes come to the conclusion that the horse is capable of going better; so we look at ways to improve next time out. Everything balances itself out; there are days when we should win and don't, days when we think we should have done better and are out of the placings, and days when we don't really deserve to do well at all, and come back with the championship.

After all, if all judges loved the same thing and held the same opinion, the sport would become very boring and gradually disappear; the variety is what showing is all about.

CHAPTER 9

Working Hunter and Working Hunter Pony Classes

No showing book would be complete without reference to the ever-popular working hunter pony/working hunter classes, and it may be more helpful to look at the general ways in which you can improve your chances of winning by obtaining higher marks in the various phases, rather than concentrate on fence construction or jumping problems. These classes are all the more interesting because the judges have to commit their views to paper with marks; as the competitors can usually see these afterwards, they are educational as well.

TYPE AND CONFORMATION

However, probably the main reason that these classes are so popular is that, unlike straightforward showing which is based purely on a judge's opinion, these classes have more the flavour of sports such as show jumping or racing where everyone stands a chance at the start since the judge's opinion must also be based on ability and performance. The type of animal is sturdier and is more likely to be able to do other jobs of work, unlike some of the prima donnas of the show ring which would die of fright and last about two seconds in the hunting field. In this day and age of ever-increasing costs, this is a consideration of some importance.

A More Versatile Type

Some of the animals to be seen in the working hunter ring are produced solely for the class; other owners use this area of showing as part of a young horse's education and have other equestrian spheres in mind such as eventing, show jumping or dressage. Horses such as Goodwill, Persian Holiday and Upton (who won the King George V Cup) have all in their early careers competed in working hunter classes. Some of our top class ponies have also excelled in other spheres: Rookery Jigsaw, WHP of the

Year in 1975, followed his success in the show ring at the Scottish Horse Show one year by cantering into the next ring and jumping against the clock in a JA regional final; when Coalport won the WHP title at Peterborough in 1976 he was already an Intermediate eventer; Paddington Bear, who is related to the show pony Midnight Shadow and regularly competed in show pony classes and working hunter pony classes, won the European Pony Event Championships in 1987; and Tracey Priest's Harden Dilwyn, runner-up at Peterborough, went on to make a name for himself in the show jumping world.

Conformation

Obviously, the first main consideration is to find a mount of the correct type with good sound conformation, otherwise no matter how well you perform over fences you will fall by the wayside in the second phase, the showing section. However, although this would seem to be a sensible and straightforward supposition, the discrepancies in the marking of conformation by some judges is truly alarming, particularly in the pony classes. Others do not use the marking system to its full advantage, sometimes giving twenty ponies marks ranging, say, from twenty to twenty-four out of thirty, which really does not help to differentiate between the ponies in the class, and often ends up with eight ponies tying for the first two placings; this is not really good enough.

Both the true working hunter and the working hunter pony must have correct conformation and must combine substance with quality – this distinguishes him from the everyday hunting misfit or riding school pony, which are often seen competing in these classes; and he must have limbs with good flat bone and short cannons which match his body-weight. A good, straight athletic movement will stand him in good stead over fences, and he should have a good level temperament to match, otherwise valuable marks for manners will be lost during the class.

Ideally, the working hunter pony is a miniature version of the successful show hunter, preferably middleweight; it is not something that would win in a top class show pony ring. Mrs Charles Cope is a past master in this field; she produced my first horse Portman Lad, and also Kingswood and Jonjo. She looks for an animal which is top of its weight category, deep and compact, and with knees and hocks well let down; she also likes to see a good movement which is straight, though not necessarily extravagant, with a fluent rhythm both on the flat and over fences.

The working hunter class is less discriminatory than the showing ones, and suits a horse which is between weights (as there is often only one open class) or simply a horse which just misses being very top class. In both horse and pony classes judges will usually forgive the odd blemish or sign of general wear and tear which in the relevant show classes would probably have been frowned upon, and may have seriously handicapped your chances. However, if the specimen which is perfect performs as well, it is commonsense that the judge will have him in preference to one which has a few faults, no matter how insignificant – so you must always strive for perfection in your quest for maximum marks.

It is amusing to hear judges who refuse to award maximum marks, stating quite indignantly that the perfect animal has not been bred, but will go to the other extreme – I feel without proper reflection – and give an animal zero! Surely the worst pony doesn't exist either and deserves a mark, even half, just for turning up! The perfect animal probably does not exist, but if an animal is outstanding in his class on the day and if circumstances dictate that he deserves full marks – even if it is solely because the next best pony has got twenty-seven out of thirty – then this is what he should have; after all, the marks' sheet belongs to the day and is not an historical document!

PERFORMANCE

Flat Work for Jumping
When you have found your perfect specimen, the next most important consideration is the flat work; not only will this pay dividends when you give your individual display and when the judge rides your horse, but flat work is the basis for complete control when jumping. After all, if your horse doesn't jump well, its excellent conformation will be superfluous and competition is so strong these days that you would be unlikely to win at a good show without jumping a clear round first of all.

You only have to look at the show jumping world to see how well schooled the horses are: they are obedient to hand and leg so they can rein back to canter with the utmost ease, stop and start at a moment's notice, and shorten and lengthen at the flick of a

Little Diamond, Working Hunter Pony of the Year, 1985, and Show Hunter Pony of the Year, 1986

switch. And the time element is just as relevant in producing working hunters as it is in any other stage of show ring production: many people are simply not patient enough to persevere with the long arduous hours of schooling necessary, and start jumping too early. Initially this does not appear to cause problems, as most animals with any talent at all will jump up to a certain height quite freely – look at youngsters playing around in the fields, who will sometimes jump out just for fun. However, when the fences become bigger and the distances more demanding, the short cuts taken in the ground work will be revealed, and the horse will start stopping, running out or catching his fences★.

Your only hope of overcoming these problems is to go back to basics again, so in the long run it is far better to do the job properly in the first place if the pony and rider are to develop a happy and successful working relationship.

Overfacing the Novice
Right from the start, it is wiser for your animal to learn correct technique over smaller fences before he tackles bigger fences and combinations, and this applies in pole work, gymnastic exercises and even loose schooling. If you overface your novice, even if by accident, and over-estimate his capabilities, the confidence which is the key to all his future progress will be lost – and just as with young jockeys, it will take a lot of sympathetic handling to regain it.

Similarly, you may, at a later date, arrive at a show with your novice and find that the course is beyond the capability of both rider and pony: do not spoil all your hard work by saying, 'Well, let's see how we cope.' Admittedly, there does come a time when your animal must occasionally be put to the test, otherwise progress cannot be made – but the decision is yours as to whether he is really ready, and on the day must not be taken lightly.

Loose Schooling
Many experts firmly believe in the value of loose schooling when jumping; it teaches the animal to think for itself and to adjust its length of stride without the added help or hindrance of a rider, and promotes confidence in its own ability. Jane Hankey, herself a talented jump jockey and whose children Hayley and Haydon often dominate the WHP classes at the major shows, believes that

---

★*The Working Hunter Pony Book* written by the Connor family contains a very good chapter on problems and is well worth reading.

you can often detect a horse's personality as well as his ability more accurately by observing him when he is jumping loose.

Grid-work

Trotting-pole work will help develop a horse's rhythm and will make him supple; it is useful at any stage of training, particularly as a change from normal work routine, and will keep your horse alert and athletic. When he is learning to jump, poles will help to regulate his stride and will guide him into a fence; placed in front of a fence, they will encourage a horse to adjust his stride before take-off, or used in combinations they will teach him to lengthen or shorten his stride where appropriate.

Obviously it is most important to place poles correctly, otherwise you are defeating the object. A good tip is to have your poles attached to a concrete block so there is less chance of knocking them crooked, and if you are by yourself it is a bind if a pole is kicked out of place and you have to jump off your horse to adjust it.

When trotting through a grid of poles, let your horse go through himself – give with your hands and allow him to stretch, and only use your legs if he starts to lose impetus. Always aim for the middle, and if he rushes, circle him away at different poles to stop him anticipating, which will make him think and teach him to respect them.

Course-building

Once your horse has learnt the correct technique over various types of fences and combinations, and has progressed to jumping a small course well, the next stage is to take him out and allow him to see as much as possible. When building courses at home the BSPS handbook and BSJA booklet will be particularly helpful when constructing combination fences, and the chapter on safety is well worth reading.

Hunting and Cross-country

Hunting and cross-country competitions will familiarise the horse with the more natural obstacles that you might hope to encounter in a good working hunter course; although even with a talented course builder it is not possible to reproduce all the natural hazards of the hunting field or, more importantly, its atmosphere, which is why you often see the star performer in the hunting field unable to excel in the confines of the ring and jump in cold blood. A little show jumping (although not against the clock at this stage) would help, and will instil discipline and accuracy as well as teaching your animal to jump in cold blood.

Most ponies and especially novices will become bolder out hunting, and will develop more ability and scope, jumping fences in a good, free, ongoing style. There is no better way to teach the novice to tackle water obstacles – much easier than having an argument with lead reins and lunge whips in the stream at home! However, your manners marks may be in jeopardy if your novice will not settle out hunting and becomes very strong; although this is often because the pony is under-bridled. Take him out cub-hunting first of all to introduce him gradually to the excitement.

The golden rule out hunting is to be cautiously well bridled, over-tacking rather than under-bridling – you can always remove the curb chain or change the running martingale to a standing, and the neck strap in both cases is useful when jumping big fences. You can also opt for practicality – for example, rubber reins are better in the hunting field than the show ring. This should not, however, be done at the expense of presentation – a high standard of turnout is a compliment to the master.

The approaches and landings in the field are usually more tricky than in the relatively flat show ring, so watch for the unexpected drop on landing. Pick a nice wide fence and always aim for the most inviting solid part with the easiest approach for take-off. Try to give yourself a clear run and never follow immediately behind another pony; as you approach the jump, keep straight, on a nice balanced stride and do not let him go flat, however exhilarating the chase, as this will teach him to rush his fences and he may peck on landing. Learn to keep him at the pace which *he* is happiest with; this will pay dividends in the ring later on. In the last few strides give him his head but without losing contact, and ride with a little more attack to lengthen the stride.

Use your discretion when tackling larger fences; do not discourage him by overfacing him and if he does refuse, try and get a lead from a more experienced pony. If he refuses unexpectedly it may be his way of letting you know that he is tired; to continue could eventually lead to falls and injuries.

By planning your winter season carefully with your novice, you can take advantage of this quieter period in preparation for the bigger summer shows. The BSPS members are indeed fortunate compared to their HIS colleagues, as they have their own winter season in which to bring on their novice WHP slowly.

WORKING HUNTER/ WHP JUMPING COURSES

No longer do WHP/working hunter courses consist of a few poles borrowed from the main ring, with a couple of trees and some straw bales; they are very often professionally built and more technical in content. Consequently it is of utmost importance to walk the course correctly – by this I mean trying to read the coursebuilder's thoughts and, since you know your horse's abilities, deciding where he is likely to make a mistake; rather than using this important time to take the dog for a walk or to give your new anorak its first public outing!

The Best Line

Your initial concern is to establish direction and find the most fluent line through the fences (especially the staggered fan type ones) as though out hunting; it is therefore essential to walk the exact track you intend to take when riding the course. Some people look for visual markers from the ringside to help them remember a certain line, and others look back after a couple of fences to check the intended line – although this should not be done when riding in the class, even if you think you may have rolled a pole – always look ahead!

Pace

The pace at which you ride the course is determined by the type of fences, the conditions underfoot and the geography and size of the ring. A horse will always respect a good solid fence, whether it is filled with greenery, plants, straw bales, water troughs, benches or flowers; these you can approach on a longer, more attacking stride than a fence with either plenty of daylight or no obvious ground line. Similarly, fences are more inviting if the wings are angled towards you rather than in a straight line with the fence itself.

The Approach

Upright or narrow fences are the hardest to jump, and you must adopt a more accurate steady stride than if jumping a spread-type fence. The true parallel fence is more difficult to jump than an ascending one or staircase fence which is more inviting since it demands less accuracy and therefore less effort. When tackling double type fences, if the distance between the two is tight or even a bounce, always try to jump out of the bottom of the first

The pace at which the competitor rides is determined by the type of fences, and by the geography of the ring, as shown here at the Royal International Horse Show

element; if the distance is longer, you can tackle the combination at a more adventurous pace.

The golden rule is always to jump straight, and aim for the centre of the fence; remember also that fences towards the entrance or collecting ring will always jump better than those away. If the going is slippery or rough, take care; sharp studs behind are ideal when the going is hard and the pace will be faster, and bigger ones for wetter conditions when it will be better to jump on a lot shorter stride.

Course Building
The ideal course is one which encourages a horse to go forwards and allows him to jump freely in a correct shape; those at the Royal and Ryedale shows are like this. Courses like Wembley are trappy and dictate the pace too much, and leave you no option but to jump on a much shorter stride. A horse ridden downhill will automatically lengthen his stride and so will need to be collected by the rider, whereas uphill the horse will collect himself.

A good course builder will be an artist with flair and imagination, as well as a scientist and a technician. He will be well aware of the standard of competitor, building a more straight-forward course for a novice and a more ambitious course for a championship like Peterborough or the Broomfield Champion-ship; for the novice, the line of fences will be simple – lots of tight turns, changes of direction and many different types of fences are for the more advanced.

He should be aiming for a certain number of clears in a given time, and looking for a rhythmical, flowing round which will encourage rather than stop an animal. The first fence should be relatively easy and not jumped away from the entrance, building up to a difficult fence not too late in the course if the entries are large – in other words, a fence which will test the rider and make the horse think. After all, a good course is one which makes a good competition and gives the competitors a sense of achievement.

JUDGING

When judging, it is better to have a reasonable number of clears and then the class can be judged as a show class – after all, it is showing. Sometimes a pony will win a class when it has had a pole down because it has jumped beautifully, placed above clear rounds which have not been in such good style. The style marks must be used sensibly: for instance, rolling a pole – especially behind – is less of a fault than if a horse crashes through the whole fence, even though the penalty mark is exactly the same. One of the hardest jobs when judging is to be accurate with your marks and with the spacings between them, and at the same time allow yourself enough scope in case the best round or pony comes into the ring last.

Some exhibitors do not like to go first, thinking that the judge will be afraid to mark high; this is nonsense, as a good judge will allow himself enough room for manoeuvre. Anyway, in some cases it pays to go early in the jumping phase to give you longer to work in for the showing phase, especially if your animal needs time to settle down after jumping.

After jumping, leave the ring as you entered, on a loose rein. Having watched a beautiful jumping round, there is nothing worse than seeing a wall-of-death gallop – in fact unless the judge has asked for a gallop at the end of this stage, it is not necessary and is only winding up your pony or horse for the next stage.

185

Style marks will definitely be lost by riders who flap about in the saddle, hissing like geese and hitting their mounts over every fence. And it is also surprising how many competitors, relieved to have finished the jumping phase, proceed to throw away their class by not concentrating on the showing phase – this particularly applies in the in-hand section when they will often stand their animals up like beached whales. In some cases the exhibits are not round and bonny since they tend to jump better when on the lean side, and therefore need to be presented all the more efficiently to look passable. Remember that marks are difficult to gain and all too easy to throw away.

These classes are going from strength to strength, and it seems they will continue to do so. As shows put on a wider range of classes to cope with the demand, some breeders are now aiming their policies towards this market; and more and more people, some from other equestrian fields, are attracted into this sport each year. It would be interesting to see the reaction of those people who instigated these classes years ago, if they could see how their ideas have developed.

CHAPTER 10

The Judging Process

JUDGES

In today's showing circle, there is a particularly keen interest in judges and their methods of judging, and exhibitors are far more aware of their different preferences than in the past; one judge may attach importance to the way of going at the expense of conformation, another may like a stronger made animal rather than a fine pretty show horse. From an exhibitor's point of view, it makes sense to know which judge likes your particular type of animal – you may be able to save the unnecessary expense of travelling hundreds of miles to show under a judge who does not.

The Judges' Panel

Show societies looking to the future are tapping this interest and encouraging more people – especially young ones – to become judges, far more so than, say, fifteen years ago, when the judges' panel appeared to be a 'closed shop'. Most societies hold 'teach-ins' and conference-type seminars which are open to potential judges as well as existing ones; these are both informative and stimulating and enable judges to keep track of the ever-improving modern-day standard, and of the many new rules which are formed as new classes are introduced. In some cases this is the only source of education available to non-horsey people who come from a town background.

Showing and judging is a continual process, and as some of our eminent judges reach the age of retirement, their places need to be filled by younger people. Some people are biased and believe that the younger generation lacks the experience to judge – often older judges who do not like to see change of any sort! In fact they underestimate the ability and intelligence of today's young people who have to be very aware and capable to succeed in our fast-thinking modern-day society.

Many of these 'youngsters' have had years of practical showing experience and know the requirements of type for the new classes; they are therefore able to provide a fresh outlook on the present-day showing scene. Those who champion the younger judges could also argue that many of the senior judges are unable to cope with the enormous number of entries, that they are twenty years behind and out of touch with the present-day standard and type.

Some people maintain that professionals showmen and breeders should be excluded from the judges' panels as they are too involved, and might favour their customers' animals and those by their own stallions. In fact professionals such as Stella Harries, Davina Whiteman and Robert Oliver – to name but a few – are a pleasure to watch when judging and do the job very efficiently; they conduct proceedings at lightning speed because they know exactly what they want and are used to all the tricks which may elude others who are not so 'on the ball'.

Those who breed horses are so used to seeing animals at various stages of growth, and are such sticklers for correct conformation, that they are equally competent when judging. As might be expected, they are especially good at dealing with the breeding classes, and particularly when judging foals.

If we do not allow these people to join the panels, we could be left with judges who are so uninvolved that they may never otherwise see a show animal from one year to the next, which could lead to a completely different opinion, and probably a bad one!

Care must be taken lest we end up with more judges than exhibitors, as sometimes appears to be the case on the Scottish BSPS panel – societies should nevertheless always keep an open door, and be prepared to look for fresh blood, especially as the number of shows increases every season. Existing judges are also restricted to the number of qualifying classes for RIHS and HOYS at which they can judge, and to a certain number of shows within a particular area.

Remember – every new judge brings another individual opinion, and this is what makes showing tick.

An Unbiased Decision

Basically, all judges are looking for the same thing – but remember, beauty is in the eye of the beholder, and judges will have different lists of priorities and will attach importance to different areas, whether it be action, limbs, feet or ride. It is only when you become a judge and officiate from the middle of the ring that you will be able to appreciate some of the results which happen, and which can at times seem strange from the ringside – this has been called 'crab corner'. For instance, a judge can only act on what he sees, and unbeknown to many ringside experts he

Professionals and breeders are a pleasure to watch when judging, and this photograph shows Liz Mansfield of the famous Rotherwood Stud judging a pony championship at the Royal Welsh Show in 1982. From left to right: Runnings Park Hill Star; Cherrington Abber; Oakley Bubbling Simone; Willow Valley Touchstone; Perryditch Temerity; Gunnerby Aalborg Elegant

has not got eyes in the back of his head and so cannot see a pony misbehaving behind his back, which may be taking place at 'crab corner'.

There is a story which elucidates this point: a friend of mine was judging a big show and in the championship was told by the steward that the 14.2hh pony was messing about behind her back. Because she had not seen this with her own eyes, she did not act on it, and duly put the 14.2hh pony champion with the 12.2hh reserve; she discovered later that the 14.2hh had not misbehaved at all, and that the 12.2hh – which would have been champion had she listened to the steward – was by the steward's stallion; in other words, he had been feeding her with incorrect information and should have been reported to the show committee.

Judges Good and Bad

Judges that are smartly dressed, organised, precise and carry an air of authority – without being aloof – and who look as though they know exactly what they are doing, inspire the exhibitor with confidence and their opinion is rarely questioned. Those who give judges a bad name will have the class in operation for a long time at the beginning, and will then pull in only two animals before sending the rest of the class into trot again; or will play to the audience, outshining the exhibits themselves.

A good judge should be relaxed and human, but at the same time should take his job seriously, bearing in mind that the value of the stock can be increased or decreased by his placings. Popular judges are those who will offer a kind word of encouragement, especially with children – although care must be taken in what is said to a young jockey, as an innocent statement can lose its meaning once out of the ring and may be misconstrued by the parents as sarcasm or flippancy. At the end of the day, it is better to keep chat down to a bare minimum, especially if the exhibitor and judge are best friends when it may be misinterpreted as favouritism.

One senior judge gave me two very sound pieces of advice: always look interested in every exhibitor, especially when watching an individual show from an exhibit at the end of the line; and never be seen to laugh during an individual show, even if it is merely at a remark made by a steward and not appertaining to anything in particular – the exhibitor may think you are laughing at him.

JUDGING

To be asked to judge is a privilege; animals which under normal circumstances would be hidden away from prying eyes at home can be examined, and any judge should be delighted when exhibitors bring good ponies into the ring for his opinion, even though it may differ from theirs. There is also the element of challenge involved, as show animals are volatile creatures and the fortunes of a class can easily change if the obvious winner misbehaves or goes lame.

Judge on the day

It is sad to see so few stars in the rings these days, although in many ways this makes the classes all that more interesting to judge, as the majority of the exhibits are of the same standard and are separated only by the merest whim or fancy. It is not good policy to prefer a show animal because it won a big show the week before or is on form, as on the day it may look a mere 'two bob'!

An animal which you have always disliked and which has probably won more than you think it deserved, should not be penalised for it – it may be the obvious winner on the day you judge. Similarly, if an animal which you have put champion on numerous occasions is not going as well as before, you must be careful not to be too hard on it – it may still be the outright champion, even on an 'off' day.

The Judge's Task

As you can see from these few examples, when judging it pays to keep an open mind; at times a judge's task is not an easy one, especially if the class is full of bad animals. However, these bad days are often outweighed by the days when everything fits into place and you drive home feeling extremely happy with the placings and with everyone in total agreement – although you must not pander to the ringside, and must always have the courage of your convictions; stand by your own judgement, even if at times it makes you unpopular. Competing on Saturday with friends and then disappointing them the next day as a judge can sometimes lead to a very lonely life.

The late Joe Masserella used to say that there are only two people you please when judging: yourself and the person who has the red rosette, and sometimes even then you are not happy, as your would-be winner has gone badly and is standing mid-way down the line.

MARKING SYSTEMS

Judging is a mental process and often a private one, yet it is surprising how many judges are unable to put their views down on paper in a marking system. This often leads to a surprise result, particularly at Wembley, especially if the two judges are split for most of the time – although you could say this is what makes Wembley unique, I suppose.

. . . at Championships

Marking systems do definitely work when a large number of judges descend on a large number of champion animals in a supreme championship. The NCPA adopted a very good system one year in which each judge had to pick his choice for supreme and reserve by giving a mark of ten and seven respectively. The total number of marks was added up and the animal with the most was obviously the winner. The system was foolproof and saved a lot of time arguing – which is often the case when judging a vast group of different types of animal, when obviously judges have different ideas. For instance, does one choose the most valuable animal in market price which may be a top class show pony, in preference to a Shetland foal? Or does one go for the animal which is best of its type? Should one strip all the animals in the supreme championship class and bring them all down to a common factor, say, correctness of conformation and action? But then again, in certain cases certain faults are more acceptable in view of the animal's intended activity, which complicates this theory somewhat – for example, a Shire horse may have a straighter shoulder as compared to a Thoroughbred.

In some cases the stallion has the advantage over a gelding because of his potential for breeding and therefore income, and anyway he usually oozes more presence, which is very important in a big championship. And a lot of people in the native pony

A big winner both in-hand and under saddle, Mr G. Hollings' 14.2hh Towy Valley Chiff Chaff, Champion at the Royal Show, 1972, and ridden by Claire Stock (Monty)

world would argue that a mare's breeding potential is more valuable than anything else – although they would agree that a mare with a foal should stand above a barren mare who has not proved her worth. However, another point worth considering when judging brood mares is, how much notice do judges take of the foals? Does a foal which on the day appears to be a bad one, question the mare's ability as a 'good mum'? Perhaps it is a first foal or a young foal, and the mare may be doing an excellent job in difficult circumstances.

There are further comparisons which may have to be contemplated: should a mature ridden pony be preferred to an in-hand youngster, the idea being that the end product/maturity should win over immaturity? – this argument is often strengthened by the fact that everyone knows that even the most glamorous youngster, especially as a foal, can make a fool of a judge as time passes on. Similarly, should a potential champion be automatically beaten, on the day, by an established one, bearing in mind the expression 'an old has-been is better than a never-will-be'? And some judges will always go for size, validating the other expression that 'a good big 'un will beat a good little 'un'.

At the end of the day the choice is endless; perhaps it is the one which simply catches the eye, the real showman with charm and appeal, which should win the overall vote.

SOUND AND WELL MANNERED?

Lameness
Perhaps the two most controversial subjects when judging are lameness and manners. If an animal appears to be lame, the judge may request the exhibitor to refer the matter to the vet officiating at the show. Once this is done and if the animal returns with an all clear, the judge should continue to assess the animal fairly – although once suspicions have been aroused it is understandable how some judges have difficulty in giving the animal the benefit of the doubt. Most senior judges would view it as a situation which must be judged as an individual case on the day.

At a show one year a judge brought back my horse after riding it for about twenty seconds and said that she suspected the horse to be uneven, and would I like to get the vet; this I duly did and the horse was passed sound. The class proceeded as normal, and at the end of the day my horse finished reserve champion to the middleweight hunter – which was surprising, since the judge never rode the horse again after bringing it back lame! This just shows how on some days you can be extremely lucky, and the gods seem to be on your side!

Manners

Bad manners in the ring from both horse and rider should not be tolerated by any judge worth his salt. Exhibitors who leave the ring without the judge's permission or arrive late without apologising should know better. Nevertheless, once a judge has allowed a late entry into the class, it should be judged as normal and should not be penalised by not winning if it deserves to, simply because it was a late arrival.

A common complaint today amongst many exhibitors is that too many judges are too fanatical about manners, to the point where they seem unable to distinguish between bad manners and high spirits – consequently they play safe, and one result of this is that many exhibits are produced to go like wooden toys, which is boring to watch and a bad thing for showing. Each case must be judged separately: for instance, exuberance in a 14.2hh pony is more acceptable because the jockey should be able to cope with a sharper pony; whereas sharpness in a lead-rein pony is not acceptable. Providing the show horse does not go berserk, it can often get away with looking as though it may explode at any moment – it is, after all the cheeky-looking horse, full of presence and with a look of the eagles, that wins the day; that extra something which a judge looks for in a show horse.

THE LAST WORD

To end, I would like to tell my favourite, true, showing story. A very well respected judge was leaving the luncheon tent after judging horse classes at quite a prestigious show, only to be confronted by an irate female exhibitor whose horse he had placed down the line.

She attacked him roundly (which has happened to us all), saying that the horse had won all over the country and that she thought he would have liked it, and towards the end of the outburst said that he wasn't fit to judge cattle. His reply was, simply, that he remembered the horse and did like it but just preferred the others above it; and if he had been asked to judge the cattle at the show that day 'You, madam, would certainly have been my champion!'

The moral being that he had the last word – and as everyone knows, the judge's decision is final!

Useful Addresses

Arab Horse Society
Windsor House
The Square
Ramsbury
Wilts SN8 2PE

British Show Hack, Cob and
   Riding Horse Association
Rookwood
Packington Park
Meriden
Warwickshire CV7 7HF

British Show Jumping
   Association
British Horse Society
Joint Measurement Scheme
all at
British Equestrian Centre
Stoneleigh
Kenilworth
Warwickshire CV8 2LR

British Show Pony Society
124 Green End Road
Sawtry
Huntingdon
Cambridgeshire PE7 5XA

Hunters Improvement Society
   (National Light Horse
   Breeding Society)
96 High Street
Edenbridge
Kent TN8 5AR

Ladies' Side-saddle Association
28 Featherbed Lane
Addington
Surrey CR0 9AE

National Pony Society
Brook House
25 High Street
Alton
Hampshire GU34 1AW

Northern Counties Pony
   Association
Lees Hall Farm
Glossop
Derbyshire SK13 9JT

Ponies Association UK
Chesham House
56 Green End Road
Sawtry
Huntingdon
Cambridgeshire PE17 5UY

Index

Page numbers in *italics* refer to illustrations.

INDEX

DAVID & CHARLES' EQUESTRIAN TITLES

Behaviour Problems in Horses · Susan McBane

Breeding and Training a Horse or Pony · Ann Sutcliffe

Champion Horses and Ponies · Pamela Macgregor-Morris

Clarissa Strachan's Young Event Horse · Clarissa Strachan

Compleat Horse · Johannes E. Flade

Dressage Begin the Right Way · Lockie Richards

Effective Horse and Pony Management   A Failsafe System · Susan McBane

Equine Fitness   The Care and Training of The Athletic Horse · Dr David Snow and Colin Vogel

Going the Distance A Manual of Long-Distance Riding · Sue Parslow

The Great Hunts · Alastair Jackson

Gymkhana! · Lesley Eccles and Linda Burgess

The Heavy Horse Manual · Nick Rayner and Keith Chivers

The Horse and The Law · Donald Cassell

Horse Breeding · Peter Rossdale

Horse Driving Trials The Art of Competitive Coachmanship · Tom Coombs

The Horse's Health From A TO Z An Equine Veterinary Dictionary (new edition) · Peter Rossdale and Susan M. Wreford

The Horse Owner's Handbook · Monty Mortimer

The Horse Rider's Handbook · Monty Mortimer

Hunting An Introductory Handbook · R. W. F. Poole

The Imperial Horse The Saga of the Lipizzaners · Hans-Heinrich Isenbart and Emil Buhrer

Keeping a Horse Outdoors · Susan McBane

Lungeing The Horse and Rider · Sheila Inderwick

A Passion for Ponies · John and Francesca Bullock

Practical Dressage · Jane Kidd

Practical Showjumping · Peter Churchill

The Riding Instructor's Handbook · Monty Mortimer

Riding and Stable Safety · Ann Brock

The Stable Veterinary Handbook · Colin J. Vogel

Transporting Your Horse or Pony · Chris Larter and Tony Jackson